You are on the right track, and I be
assist many people in their journey

MOST REVEREND HARRY J. FLYNN, DD
Archbishop Emeritus of Saint Paul and Minneapolis

Thom Winninger has gained deep insights into the inner life and shares not just the lessons, but the process that can be used to dive deep into your own story. If you're ready to get out of the boat and live life as God intended us to live it, I recommend you read this engaging and interactive book.

MARK SANBORN
Author of *The Fred Factor: How Passion in Your Work and Life Can Turn the Ordinary into the Extraordinary, You Don't Need a Title to Be a Leader: How Anyone, Anywhere, Can Make a Positive Difference,* and *The Encore Effect: How to Achieve Remarkable Performance in Anything You Do*

If you've ever awaked in the middle of the night wondering, "Is this all there is for me?," Winninger's work leads you to life-changing answers. Using everyday scenarios, Scripture, prayer suggestions, piercing personal questions, and reflections on everyday reality, Winninger invites readers to join him on a journey to discover their life purpose. Highly recommended for the seasoned and the seeker.

DIANNA BOOHER
Author of *The Voice of Authority: 10 Communication Strategies Every Leader Needs to Know* and *Your Signature Work: Creating Excellence and Influencing Others at Work*

Thom Winninger not only "gets" out of the boat, he lives there! I have known this inspiring man for almost a generation. I trust him...and so can you. Take his message to heart and let his inspiration touch your life. You and our world will be better because you did so.

JIM CATHCART
Author of *Relationship Selling*

With profound purpose and passion, Thom strikes with intentionality and experiences the probing of our hearts. We are challenged to go deeper in the well of our giftedness in this treatise written from the depths of personal experience and the empowering of the Holy Spirit. What an enigma!

NAOMI RHODE
Christian leader and cofounder of SmartHealth

Get
Out
of the
Boat

Get
Out
of the
Boat

Discover the
Meaning of
Your Life

Liguori
LIGUORI, MISSOURI

Thomas J.
Winninger

Imprimi Potest:
Thomas D. Picton, C.Ss.R.
Provincial, Denver Province
The Redemptorists

Published by Liguori Publications
Liguori, Missouri
To order, call 800-325-9521
www.liguori.org

Copyright © 2010 Thomas J. Winninger

Library of Congress Cataloging-in-Publication Data

Winninger, Thomas J.
  Get out of the boat : discover the meaning of your life / Thomas J. Winninger.
     p. cm.
  ISBN 978-0-7648-1881-3
 1. Spirituality--Catholic Church. 2. Spiritual life--Catholic Church. 3. Meaning (Philosophy)--Religious aspects--Christianity. I. Title.
  BX2350.65.W56 2009
  248.4--dc22

                                                              2009042159

Liguori Publications, a nonprofit corporation, is an apostolate of the Redemptorists. To learn more about the Redemptorists, visit Redemptorists.com.

Printed in the United States of America

14 13 12 11 10   5 4 3 2 1

First edition

Acknowledgments

Thanks to...

...my Lord, for calling me to get out of my boat so I could find joy in a life lived in faith while dealing with the world rather than living in the world while hoping faith will be part of it;

...Kay Harkness, for her editorial assistance with the flow of this book;

...my editor and daughter, Ginny, for bringing faith and the spirit to this work;.

...LeAnn Thieman, speaker, friend, and coauthor of the *Chicken Soup for the Soul* series, who led me to Liguori Publications;

... to my friend in Christ, Jim Murphy (1958–2009), an inspiration to this book in his short life simply by demonstrating how to encounter Jesus every day

...Liguori editorial director Jay Staten, for helping me to understand the value of my journey to others;

...Ignatius, for turning his challenges into the process of taking life's big questions to the Lord;

...all Jesuits, who remind me daily that we are a soul with a body, not a body who just happens to have a soul;

...Naomi Rhode and Charlie Tremendous Jones, friends in Christ who inspired me with the never-give-up attitude faith demands;

...my parents, Larry and Betty Winninger, for nurturing the seed of belief within me at an early age;

…Archbishop Harry Flynn, whose inspiration as a spiritual man and retreat master drew me to the permanent diaconate;

…Sister Joan Tubety, spiritual counselor, who cheered me on when the game of life was tied;

…Giovanni Liver, who walked with me as I encountered Christ;

…C. S. Lewis, Dietrich Von Hildebrand, John Eldredge, Karol Wojtyla, Thomas Aquinas, and Augustine, for their written words of inspiration to the clarity of truth.

My love and appreciation to my beautiful bride of 29 years, Lynne, and our children Ginny, Kate, Nicholas, and Alex for being there though the ebbs and flows of life in the boat.

Dedication

*To all who feel trapped in busy lives filled
with activity but without meaning.*

Contents

Foreword

Face to Face

As I was walking beside the Sea of Galilee on a warm summer afternoon, I saw two brothers, James, son of Zebedee, and his brother, John. They were in a small fishing boat with their father, preparing their nets. I called them, and immediately they left the boat and their father and followed me. They got out of the boat. As I called them to join me, they didn't say we'll think about it. I hadn't asked them to think about it. I didn't say that I would return in a couple of days to see what they had decided. I asked them to get out of the boat and walk with me. At that very moment, we began a journey that would last for all eternity.

Walking together along the sandy shoreline, the two brothers questioned me about life, the purpose for life, the purpose of their lives. They asked me why certain things happen to one person and not to another. Why some are successful and others aren't successful. They asked why some people are happy and others aren't happy. They asked me why God seems to punish some and not punish others. They asked me why my Father doesn't seem to answer their prayers. They asked me why some die so young yet others live to be old. They asked me how to find meaning in life. They asked me what is important in life. They asked me why some suffer so much. They asked, and they asked, and they asked.

I showed them how to find the answers to their questions. I told them that God my Father doesn't place as much emphasis on the role one plays in life, but rather, what kind of relationship one has with me. Ultimately, how one lives that relationship in every aspect of the role one plays.

If I ask you to get out of the boat, will you have the confidence to leave everything in your life to me? If I ask you to get out of yourself, your world, and everything you're doing that seems so important, will you want time to think about it? Perhaps you might say, "No, thanks. I'm getting along just fine. I have a lot of things that I'm working on; maybe someday."

I'm asking you to get out of your boat. Take this time and walk with me. Tell me about yourself. Ask me to help you understand your life. Ask me about the purpose of your life. Ask me about your relationships. Ask me any question you want. I'll show you, as I showed James and John, how to find the answers to your questions.

Deep inside your very being, you already hold all the questions and all the answers. When I created you, not only did I give you the purpose to your life, I created you with the answers to your unique life. Get out of your boat! It will be most significant decision of your life!

SEE MATTHEW 4:18–22

DEAR FRIEND,

    Each day we get the call to get out of the boat, leave behind what we're doing, and put our confidence in Christ. Jesus speaks to us just as openly as he spoke to James and John on the day he called them to be his disciples. Some accept the call because something happens that doesn't make sense. Some get out of the boat because their lives take a turn for the worse, and they need God's help. Some respond because a friend or loved one dies or because a relationship with someone they love falls apart. Some respond because their jobs aren't working out. In every case, there is an initiator. It can be a person, a situation, or an unresolved action that finally brings us away from our self-dependence. It makes no difference who or what is the initiator. It's a wake-up call to seek a deeper relationship with the most important part of our lives. It's a call to get out of our boat and spend time developing a relationship with Jesus.

Whether or not these initiators are a reality for you, there is a reason that you're reading this letter. I assume that wherever you are on this journey of life, there is something calling you deeper into the meaning of things, deeper into the why of things, deeper into an understanding of what the journey of life has in store for you.

Unfortunately, many of us live our lives like a shallow river, flowing up or down depending on the rain. We flow passively through life, controlled by our environment. But those whose lives are like a well, deep and refreshing, collect water as a source of life for themselves and others. When drought comes, they can overcome the dryness and continue to support their and others' journeys and the journeys of those around them.

Getting out of the boat—getting out of our own preoccupation with ourselves—gives us the ability to seek the depth of relationship with Christ. We become like the well, which gives us the strength of life and the purpose that sustains us, no matter what happens on our journey to salvation.

We're all taking a trip. For this trip, we take care to do all the things in order to ensure a good start. The bags are packed. The car is filled up. Everyone's seat belts are buckled. Everything is ready. Then we just sit there, going nowhere. What kind of journey it this? Of course, when we take a real trip, we have a destination. If we go on a vacation, we choose a place that attracts us. Then we start making plans. All of the planning contributes to our arrival at that location.

How strange that we live our daily lives so differently from planning a trip. We don't pick our destinations. We just get up every day, pour the coffee, and sit in our boat, mending our nets; then we launch the boat to see which direction life, the wind, and the current will take us. Without direction, we get lost, resulting in a journey that is unsatisfactory and unfulfilling. We take risks out of line with our life's purpose. We make mistakes. We listen to the wrong people. We let our weaknesses rather than our strengths drive our decisions. If we have any relationship with Christ at all, it's built on a superficial wish list of things that we want, rather than on a relationship with Christ motivated by the desire for a deeper understanding of our purpose and Christ himself.

Christ challenges us to get out of the boat and walk with him, for he is our destination—salvation is the destination. Only in this way, will the route become obvious. Only in this way, will we come to know the real purpose for our lives. Finally, choices and opportunities to fulfill the purpose of our souls will reveal themselves to us. What talents have we been given to fulfill the purpose? What route are we meant to take? Who are we supposed to take the trip with?

We're all well aware of the impulses that come to us from the world about us. We physically react to people, entertainment, emotion, or physical attractiveness. We live on the surface. In our humanness, we're attracted to so many things. Additionally, we're given free will, allowing us to make decisions for the wrong reasons, leading us in the wrong directions. When, if ever, was the last time you looked into your inner mirror and asked yourself, *What should I be doing? What will make me truly satisfied with my life? Why aren't things working for me? Why do I seem to make stupid decisions? Why don't I ever get ahead? Why don't my relationships work out the way I want?*

Most of us live our lives surrounded by everyday junk. We speed down the street, tossing lunch into our mouths, listening to music we don't understand. In the meantime, we're talking on the phone to someone we don't care much about, and giving hand signs to the poor person in the next car! The truth is, while we're angry with what's going on around us, there is a voice inside of us crying out, saying, "Hey, you missed it! You've missed it!"

Believe me, it's not just Exit 24 that we've missed.

The call for all of us is to get out of the boat, so as *not* to miss it. The call asks us to understand that the real secret to where we're going and the real purpose we need to bring to our lives is already there. Once we get out of the boat, we'll come to a deeper understanding of ourselves and will begin to ask the right questions.

My entire life has been a journey of learning the hard way—my way. I've accomplished a lot of things that most people would judge as successful, but to me it has all been just a lot of stuff. Recently, I have come to discover a truth: if whatever we accomplish isn't based on the purpose for which we were created, we'll never gain real joy in our lives. The deeper our relationship with Christ, the better the questions we'll bring to that relationship, and in turn, the better will be the answers we receive.

I have spent most of my life asking the wrong questions. Perhaps because I was so busy doing what I wanted with the gifts that God gave me, I was afraid to ask the big questions. Rather, I would ask for the things that fulfilled my journey, things that would fulfill my success goals. The person who isn't afraid will ask, *Why do I exist? Why was I created? What's the purpose for my life? What gifts do I have that I should act upon? What should I be doing that will apply my gifts for the greater honor and glory of God?*

As I became more successful, I spent more time around other equally successful people. I found that the people who had accumulated the most seemed to be the unhappiest; yet, the people who had accumulated the least seemed to have the most joy! Why is that? I believe the answer is found in what each of us is made for—the purpose for our lives.

The answer isn't in how much we've accumulated or how successful we've become. It's found in how we've been able to apply our talents, our gifts, to our life purpose. Psalm 139 says God knows us better than we can ever know ourselves:

O Lord, you've searched me and known me.
You know when I sit down and when I rise up;
  you discern my thoughts from far away.
You search out my path and my lying down,
  and are acquainted with all my ways.
Even before a word is on my tongue,
  O Lord, you know it completely.
You hem me in, behind and before,
  and lay your hand upon me.
Such knowledge is too wonderful for me;
  it is so high that I cannot attain it.

Where can I go from your spirit?
  Or where can I flee from your presence?
If I ascend to heaven, you are there;
  if I make my bed in Sheol, you are there.
If I take the wings of the morning
  and settle at the farthest limits of the sea,
even there your hand shall lead me,
  and your right hand shall hold me fast.
If I say, 'Surely the darkness shall cover me,
  and the light around me become night',
even the darkness is not dark to you;
  the night is as bright as the day,
  for darkness is as light to you.

For it was you who formed my inward parts;
  you knit me together in my mother's womb.
I praise you, for I am fearfully and wonderfully made.

Wonderful are your works;
that I know very well.
  My frame was not hidden from you,
when I was being made in secret,
  intricately woven in the depths of the earth.
Your eyes beheld my unformed substance.
In your book were written
  all the days that were formed for me,
  when none of them as yet existed.
How weighty to me are your thoughts, O God!
  How vast is the sum of them!
I try to count them—they are more than the sand;
  I come to the end—I am still with you.
Search me, O God, and know my heart;
  test me and know my thoughts.
See if there is any wicked way in me,
  and lead me in the way everlasting.

PSALM 139 1-18; 23-24

Introduction

Seven Encounters With Christ

We must be reminded that when we were created, before we were born, God planted in us the purpose for our life. He loves us so much that he gifted us with a purpose from the moment of conception. So many of us go through life never seeing or believing our purpose. You have discovered a desire to understand your purpose. We all have this desire. This desire comes with our created nature. It's a desire for holiness.

I'm not promising that you'll instantly change your life or find immediate joy, but you'll set your life on a better course to the most fulfilling destination. You'll discover that it's first through faith, not through activity, that you'll find the meaning of your life.

In Philippians 3:14–15, we read that Paul strove to get closer to God every moment of his life:

I press on towards the goal for the prize of the heavenly call of God in Christ Jesus. Let those of us then who are mature be of the same mind; and if you think differently about anything, this too God will reveal to you.

We come to know two things. First, God is with us every moment of our lives. Second, we can discern his voice by paying attention to those things that he places in front us—the good and the bad. That's right, the good and the bad. In order to hear his voice, we must pay attention. To pay attention we must be "quiet." We must compose ourselves into a frame of mind that shuts out the radio and the television, the computers, the video games, and everything else that tends to a draw us away from a posture of attention. In the quietness of those moments, we must learn to ask ourselves serious questions:

- What really makes me happy?

- What gives me true joy?

- What have I done in my life that makes me sad?

*- What gifts do I have that, for one reason or another, seem
to work better than anything else?*

- How does God reveal himself to me in my daily activities?

This isn't about bolts of lightning or crashes of thunder. It not
about the water parting or a sudden a huge wave hitting your boat
that wakes you up to your purpose in life and gives you a deeper faith.

But it could be.

The Secret of Purpose

"We come to know God by knowing ourselves better through Jesus
Christ. We come to know others by coming to know God through
Jesus Christ. We come to meaning through purpose!"

Tribute to Ignatius Loyola

Born in the work of Ignatius Loyola, this process of reflection follows a style of prayer used for centuries. Over five hundred years
ago, Ignatius founded an order of priests called the Jesuits. His
life experience exemplifies the human awakening—he got out of
his boat. Spending many years headed in a self-guided direction
defined by power, wealth, and world domination, he ultimately
found a life filled with utter emptiness and lack of purpose.

Through God's hand, he came to seek a process directing him
into a deep relationship with Christ and an understanding of his
true life purpose. Ignatius' revelation identified the truth about the
significance of individual purpose ultimately providing a joyful,

fulfilling, and meaningful life. He discovered that a clear understanding of our purpose allows for easier life choices, in turn keeping us on track with who we're really meant to be. Ignatius found that getting out of the boat required shutting out the interruptions of the world, in order to hear the voice whispering within him. Identifying this voice as God incarnate in Jesus Christ, Ignatius learned to recognize the voice and understand its role in his life. As he developed a deep connection with Christ and came to know his purpose, Ignatius labeled this process discernment. From his insights, he formulated the Spiritual Exercises.

Offered herein are the Spiritual Exercises captured in a simple format, simply called in-the-world discernment. Practicing this process of discernment on a daily basis helps us to get to know ourselves, so that we can encounter God through Jesus Christ revealed in our very nature, God revealed in our gifts, and God revealed in our experiences.

It has often been mistakenly assumed that a person with most knowledge of the Bible is most obedient to God's commands. Mere knowledge doesn't develop a relationship with Christ; rather, it's knowledge followed by action. The stronger our actions in faith grow, the better we know ourselves, the easier we'll know Jesus Christ and the unique purpose God has created for our lives.

Purpose will bring meaning and true joy. It's not just about happy moments, it's not about thinking, *This is the greatest thing that has ever happened to me!* Rather, it's an energy absorbed through both the good and the bad experiences of life. Through this relationship with Christ, we open our hearts to the deeper effect of grace. We come to feed from the spring of energy that is provided for us—discovering the gift of grace and flowing abundance of joy. Access to this life-giving spring comes when our actions and decisions are congruent with our created purpose—your created purpose.

The Process

Although at times a great help and highly recommended, walling yourself up in a retreat house isn't the answer to the process. The process doesn't ask us to take ourselves out of the world physically, but to discover how in the world we can develop a relationship with Jesus Christ. It's about *poustinia*, a Russian verb meaning stillness in a busy world. *Poustinia* calls us to mentally remove ourselves from the world. *Poustinia* opens us to presence in the immediate moment, in order to hear Jesus speaking to us from the middle of traffic, a hectic schedule, or a crowded room.

Most of us aren't called to the ascetic life of Saint Anthony the Hermit. God calls most of us to serve him in the world, in our families, in our workplace, in our faith communities. Living our faith daily through action will finally bring answers to the big questions we ask ourselves about life and purpose.

Daily Pattern for Encounters With Christ

Two exercises, one in the morning and one in the evening, will define each day.

The Morning Reflections involve a conversation with Christ, a brief reading, and a reflection on questions related to the reading. After a period of time to think about how you see God working in your life, you'll be asked to apply the answers to those questions related to where you've been, where you are, and where you think you need go.

At the end of each day the Examen, as Ignatius calls it, provides a period of time to look at how God, through your relationship with Jesus Christ, made himself known to you that day.

- *When in your day did you feel insights into your purpose?*
- *What experiences drew you to a new understanding?*
- *What did you do in the world?*
- *How did you interact with the world?*
- *What change did you observe in yourself today?*
- *Did you experience a special insight? What?*
- *Did you bring out the best in someone else? How?*
- *Did you make a decision on the basis of one of your strengths? What?*

Morning Reflection: Encounter With Christ

The seven-step structure is meant to take you to a deeper level of self-understanding.

Step One: *Pause—Gain Interior Peace.* Find a place where you can be by yourself and seek the stillness within you. Let go of all the stresses of the coming day.

Step Two: *Enter—Practice Dwelling in the Presence of Jesus— Face to Face.* Think about the infinite openness of God.

Step Three: *Begin With Silent Prayer.* A prayer is included in each daily encounter.

Step Four: *Reflect—Use Your Imagination.* Place yourself within Scripture. Imagine yourself in the story.

Step Five: *Make Your Requests Known.* Talk to God. Let him know what you need.

Step Six: *Engage Jesus in Conversation.* Ask questions.

Step Seven: *Offer Thanks—Closing Prayer.* Thank Jesus for this opportunity to spend time in his presence.

Evening Examen: Encounter With Christ

The Evening Examen follows a similar pattern to the Morning Reflection, including finding interior peace, practicing being in the presence of Jesus, offering a prayer, using your imagination, making your requests known, engaging in conversation with Jesus, and giving thanks. A significant part of your spiritual health, the Examen should become a part of the rest of your life.

The Examen doesn't follow a regimen of rules or a specific list; however, it does ask you to pay attention to your relationship with Jesus and the way your personality, your strengths and weaknesses, and your likes and dislikes affect your day. Somewhat similar to an examination of conscience, it asks you to identify where you moved close to Jesus and where you moved away after each day.

This type of reflection helps us to understand ourselves, because we're able to recognize on a daily basis how we react to situations and impulses. Conditioning ourselves to identify our actions allows us to react effectively to God's call in our lives.

During the Evening Examen, you'll be presented with questions:

- *What has been most important to me today?*
- *What did I accomplish today that made me feel good about myself?*
- *Where did I feel like God instructed me?*
- *Who has shown me God's love today?*
- *Whom did I hurt?*

Next, you'll be presented with meditations. Review your day slowly:

- *What stands out?*
- *Where did I feel energized?*
- *What did I regret?*
- *What caused me pain?*
- *What little thing happened that caught my attention?*

Review the following steps to the Examen to gain a better understanding of the spiritual exercise:

Step One
Pause—Gain Interior Peace

With an understanding that the quiet moments most often reveal God's voice, separate yourself from the interruptions around you and focus your attention on the stillness within. Find a comfortable position and relax. Close your eyes or focus on a single object for a brief period of time.

Step Two
Enter—Practice Dwelling in the Presence of Jesus—Face to Face

Imagining yourself sitting with Jesus, draw your mind to quiet as you look into the depths of his eyes. Dwell on your yearning for self-understanding, and ponder why your life may not be where you think it needs to be. Imagine Jesus tenderly listening to you with a depth of understanding impossible to comprehend. He offers no judgment, no threat, and no tension. God in the person of Jesus Christ is sitting next to you in this very room. Leaning forward, he listens intently to everything you're thinking. He asks you questions that don't threaten, but instead encourage you to share at the deepest level.

Step Three
Begin With Silent Prayer

Give me peace O Lord, and help me to understand your plan for me. Envelop me in a peace that allows insight and helps me to understand what you're saying to me. Help me to understand the meaning of my existence. What did you create me for? Guide me to your energy, and light the path you wish for me to seek. O, Lord, I'm here to listen. I'm seeking to understand. Thank you for being here with me. Amen.

Step Four
Reflect—Use Your Imagination

Place yourself in the situation of the Scripture passage. Placing yourself in Scripture will become a daily pattern for these moments of prayer. Picture yourself as a person in the crowd as Jesus walks by. Think of yourself sitting around the table in the Upper Room. What do you see? What do you smell? What kind of feelings do you have? Fully immerse your senses into this situation.

Step Five
Make Your Requests Known

After reading the reflection and imagining yourself in the presence of Christ, write a brief answer to each question. The answers are yours and yours alone. Give yourself the freedom to write whatever comes to mind. If you need more space, use additional paper. Let your mind wrap around your feelings and the understanding of where you are in terms of the question. At times, you may feel the urge to write your conversation with Jesus. Be sure to date the paper. While you're answering a question, if another comes to you, feel free to write it down. You'll find that over time, your ability to create your own questions will bring you to a deeper level of reflection.

Step Six
Engage Jesus in Conversation

Now ask Jesus, sitting next to you, any questions you posed or couldn't answer yourself to your conversation with Jesus. Ask him for insights or affirmation to the ideas that you wrote down in your journal. Ask him to provide you with any additional reflections that will bring you to a deeper understanding of where you are in relationship to today's reflections.

Step Seven
Offer Thanks—Closing Prayer

At the close of your reflection, ask Jesus for special grace today. Ask him for the grace to recognize his voice and his role in your life. Finally, give Jesus thanks for the time spent together today.

Be acutely aware of your journey over the next few days. The process will ebb and flow for you; you can't expect each day to be immensely better or more insightful than the last. Some days, there will be great insight for you. You'll walk away feeling refreshed and at peace. You'll feel the answers to your questions have opened the world to you. Other days, you may feel that the reflection and Examen were a waste of time, with no gained insights or answers. Stay dedicated to the process; don't become discouraged. Over time, you'll find that the process becomes easier, and your relationship with Jesus will go deeper than you ever imagined possible. Eventually, your heart will find peace in answers to life's big questions, and you'll find a deeper meaning to the purpose of your life.

Face to Face

A dark, black night, my disciples gathered in the Upper Room. Devastated by the events a few days ago in Calvary, the element of fear filling the room suffocated each person sitting around the table. Their minds were drowning in thoughts of what may happen to them now that I was gone. Doubt crept into their minds as they wondered whether all the sacrifice, time, and energy had been a waste. Had they squandered the last three years of their lives dreaming about paradise, talking about paradise, preaching about paradise? Thomas wasn't among them. Always busy with things, he went back to filling his life with stuff now that I was gone. On most occasions, he had made lists of things that he just had to get done and was often late joining me.

You're very similar to my disciples. You have actually spent very little time with me. Yes, you attend Mass and pray once in a while, but your mind is frequently distracted by all the things that you need to get done, removing your focus from me at church and in prayer. Like my disciples, you, too, wonder if your time spent in prayer or at mass is a waste because you fail to see the difference it makes in your life. Remember, my disciples had difficulty staying awake in the garden to pray with me the night the soldiers arrested me.

No time with me is wasted. Your life is wasted without me. No matter what you do, your role in life solely depends on the relationship you have with me. You have spent years in the carpenter shop; now, I want you to go to the desert to learn about yourself. The years spent in the carpenter shop have brought your talents to light but not to The Light, not to The Light of my purpose for you. Becoming self-indulged, you realize that your accomplishments haven't brought total fulfillment. Spend these coming days with me. What do you have to lose? You have everything to gain. Be present. Eat bugs. Bring straw to the manger. Do not be afraid like my disciples in the Upper Room. You know that I have come to save you; I'll never leave you. Paradise awaits you at the end of our journey. The world needs everything I created you for, but in all I gave you I never got you. Taking the talents and gifts, you went your way. You're now on the road to Damascus; you are my Paul. I'll open your eyes and show you how to really live. I'll show you where the battle of life must be fought. You appreciate so many things, but possess so few of them. You have wasted time, and it hasn't been with me. Please waste some time with me! You'll soon realize that no time you spend with me is never wasted. I'll show you who you really are. I'll show you what I want you to do for me.

"Lord, what will you have me do?"

SEE ACTS 9:6

Shaping Your Frame of Mind

To find success in your efforts to get deeper into your faith, into your relationship with Jesus and closer to true purpose, you must understand some basic principles. Foundational personal characteristics will help you prepare and shape your frame of mind.

Receptivity

Many times we think we're being receptive to God, when we're really just asking him to rescue us. We find ourselves building our lives around our goals and then asking God to participate. "This is what I want to do; now please help me out, OK?" or we get ourselves into a predicament and then pray, "Please, God, make this better" or "God save me from this!"

During the process of deepening our faith and getting to know our purpose, receptivity will allow us to put what we hear first, rather than what we want. When I have truly blocked the world out during the reflective periods of my life, I have found that I hear things I knew all along but which weren't clear at the time. It's as if I knew I should have done that, but now ask myself why didn't I do it? I was on my own agenda.

Fear of losing control of our lives often becomes an obstacle to receptivity. It leaves us with a feeling of vulnerability. God incarnate in Jesus Christ created you. He knows you and your desires better than you know yourself. He would never ask anything of you that would leave you empty or lost. He wants your happiness, your joy. He will challenge you to be vulnerable and to surrender yourself to openness and receptivity. If you truly let go of your fears, what could it lead you to?

Don't be frustrated if this doesn't come easily during these early days. You've spent all these years ordering your life according to what you thought you wanted. You designed your life around an infatuation with the world and the things that teased and sensitized your passions to the point of disordering your affections.

Honesty

As a part of our human nature, we become defensive when feeling attacked or criticized for something we have done or failed to do. We make up excuses for the way we are; such as, lack of education, upbringing, or lack of opportunities. We say things like, "I didn't get my degree because my parents didn't encourage me. I didn't have opportunities like the others." Or, "I didn't get the job I really wanted." As you listen to these excuses, realize that the first person pronoun, "I," keeps presenting itself. You must come to realize that there is no longer an "I" in the process. God replaces the "I" and the "me."

Honesty with ourselves will provide us the opportunity to identify the real obstacles in our lives that are preventing us from achieving fulfillment. Maybe a long-ago event so gravely affected your self-perception that you've spent your life trying to prove that you're better than the person in the scenario.

For example, an insignificant thing in retrospect, my teacher and parents held me back in third grade. This hiccup in my youth affected the way I tried to prove myself for much of my life, telling myself each day that I deserved to be respected. I promised myself that I would never let myself fail, and much of my motivation since has been purely for peer acceptance. Many of those years were spent accomplishing things that brought compliments, recognition, and acceptance, even if they weren't things I necessarily enjoyed doing. In the end, I found neither real fulfillment nor real joy.

Prayer

The basic foundation of this journey is prayer. Over time, you'll find that a conversation with Jesus deepens your reflection and self-understanding. Taking you out of the world, prayer brings you into an intimate and personal connection with God and his only begotten son. Throughout this process, suggestions of prayers or ideas that will assist you in your prayer journey are offered.

Praying isn't the main objective. Our goal isn't just to pray for the sake of praying; we're working to build a prayer lifestyle. Each and every day of our lives is a sacred prayer. Incorporating your actions into prayer unlocks the secret to a deeper faith. Although there will be times of despair in your life, and you may feel Jesus isn't listening, praying will help you work through the problems and the suffering faster than anything else. When you feel your problems weighing heavily on you, and the last thing you desire to do is pray, pray anyway. Ask for insight, ask for help, ask for the strength to bear the moment, or simply sit in silence with the Lord.

Prayer has no time, only a place. Find a place in your daily routine to semi-disconnect from the world around you. Many people pray in their cars, although this won't work if you're making a mad dash to get somewhere. Think instead about spending a few moments in the parking lot before heading into work. Use this moment to reflect, to say a few words, to make a request of God, to thank him for all the wonderful things in your life. Listen to the voice inside you providing insights as part of this mystery called life.

Commitment

Anyone who has attempted an exercise program realizes the first few days are the most difficult, relying heavily on endurance in order to remain committed. Similarly, you might find it difficult to set aside time to go through the Reflection in the morning and the Examen in the evening, but each completed day will become easier. Just like those who exercise every day, you'll find Encounters With Christ become a necessity every day. It will make you feel good, and without it, your day will seem incomplete. These activities will become part of your life, rather than something you "do" in your life.

Discernment

Saint Ignatius Loyola found that one of the most significant, basic personal characteristics to a deeper spiritual life is discernment. This pure process allows us to identify our life experiences, skills, and talents God has gifted. Then it guides us into a deeper comprehension of ourselves and of the purpose for those skills, talents, and experiences. Discernment requires time and commitment.

The first part of discernment requires you to identify the choices you make in your day-to-day life.

- Why do you say "yes" to some things and "no" to others?
- What are the consequences of those decisions?
- What are the motivations behind those decisions?
- Is it laziness?
- Is it recognition?
- Is it money?
- Is it desire?
- What is the main reason you do what you do?

Second, we recognize the presence of an inner conscience, operating at a variety of levels in different people. A conscience not only identifies blatant right and wrong, it also provides us with a keen sense of judgment and allows us to make good decisions. Unfortunately, today's society tends to weaken and destroy our consciences. We're numb and blind to the way people dress, the language they use, and the references they make. Things we used to think were sinful, we now just blindly accept. We tend to feel attracted to certain ways of life because society has conditioned us to be. To see our lives purely and clearly, our consciences must become increasingly acute during the discernment process.

The third stage of discernment involves consolation. An increase in faith, hope, and love stems from a level of detachment from things around us. The ability to let go of the extra stuff in our lives gives us clarity and allows us to make decisions based purely in faith, hope, and love, untainted by outside motivations.

He said, 'Go out and stand on the mountain before the LORD, for the LORD is about to pass by.' Now there was a great wind, so strong that it was splitting mountains and breaking rocks in pieces before the LORD, but the LORD was not in the wind; and after the wind an earthquake, but the LORD was not in the earthquake; and after the earthquake a fire, but the LORD was not in the fire; and after the fire a sound of sheer silence. When Elijah heard it, he wrapped his face in his mantle and went out and stood at the entrance of the cave. Then there came a voice to him that said, 'What are you doing here, Elijah?'"

1 KINGS 19:11–13

The Four Principles

Ignatius understood that to effectively move ahead on any decision, one must build a strong foundation around mental attitude and physical stamina. Ignatius built his foundation on four principles:

Principle One

We're created to praise, reverence, and serve God our Lord and by these means achieve eternal well-being.

Ignatius designed the first principle of the foundation to aim us toward the discovery of a meaning in our lives bigger than we are. This idea recognizes that our existence serves purpose and follows something built into our creation. Our purpose is to live a belief and a way of life that fulfills our unique calling. We must come to choose the belief that God created us. He created us to praise him, to reverence him, and to serve his desires here on earth.

Principle Two

Everything in the world is provided to help us pursue eternal well-being.

If something helps us serve our created purpose, we must use it. If something hinders us, we shouldn't use it. Ignatius brought us to a simple focus on a daily openness to recognize those things upon which we can build a foundation, a purpose for our lives, and to steer clear of those things that detract or distract from our calling.

We could draw a line down the center of a page. For each half-hour increment, we could identify whether we did something we thought was in line with our purpose in life, or something that wasn't in line with our purpose in life. From my experience, it seems that even if you don't know your purpose yet, you still have the ability to identify which activities give honor and glory to God and strengthen your relationship with Jesus Christ.

Principle Three

We must place less emphasis on external matters such as sickness or health, wealth or poverty, fame or obscurity, and long or short life.

In the Old Testament, many believed sickness symbolized a lack of success or a curse from God. Some hold that belief even today. Ignatius, however, challenges us to think in a different way. He recognizes that joy and pain benefit and enrich our lives, rather than represent judgment or punishment from God. We have the opportunity to discover strength through the positive things that happen in our lives and through the negative things in our lives. God gifts each of these in different ways.

Principle Four

We should want only the purpose we were created for.

As we look around, we find many unhappy or dissatisfied people. No matter what they accomplish, there still remains something to be desired. Then again, is life meant to completely fulfill us?

We exist on earth with the ultimate purpose of getting to paradise. If everything on earth fulfilled us, why would we have any desire for the life hereafter? We often measure our lives in terms of our success based on employment, money, property, education, and skills. God, on the other hand, measures us based upon the relationship we have with his son, Jesus Christ, and the decisions we make as a result of that relationship. Do we use what we have been given as an instrument for what we're created, to reverence and to serve? Or do we use it as a vehicle to supply our self-imposed happiness?

First Encounter

Build Your Life on Praise, Reverence, and Service

Morning Reflection

Pause—Gain Interior Peace

In the quiet moments, we hear God's voice. We need to separate ourselves from interruptions and mental distractions. Sit quietly by yourself. Listen to the voice within. Close your eyes for a few moments or focus your eyes on a single object for a brief time.

Enter—Practice Dwelling in the Presence of Jesus—Face to Face

Place yourself in the presence of the Lord. Imagine you're sitting with Jesus. Think about how you yearn to understand yourself and reflect on why your life isn't where it needs to be. Imagine Jesus speaking to you and listening to what you're saying. He offers no judgment, no threat, no tension. God in the person of Jesus Christ is sitting next to you in this very room.

He leans forward as he speaks to you…

Be still. You have all the time in the world. I'm here with you every moment. Do not let the world overwhelm you. It's not worth it. When you hold the ultimate objective of life in your mind and heart, things get simple and life gets easier. The ultimate objective, the higher the call, the simpler the truth, and the more clarity you'll find. The higher call is a relationship with me, not with your career. Our relationship is and always will be the ultimate call.

There is nothing wrong with being busy. Paul was busy, Aquinas was busy, Augustine was busy, John Paul was busy, but their activity was focused on their relationship with me. They weren't like rivers flowing shallowly into all the crevices of life; rather, they were deep wells retaining water for refreshment of those who came for nourishment. You spend so much time doing stuff. Put the stuff in the closet and get it out of sight. Trust me. It will feel good. Keep me in view. Only then will you discover the desires I have placed in your heart. You'll recognize them by the way I disclose them to you. When you knock, I'll open. Bring it all to me. Bring me your questions, bring me your frustrations, bring me your anger, bring me your failings and I'll show you love, I'll show you forgiveness; I'll show you true joy. The answers to who you're to be and what you're to do will be obvious, but you must remain still. Be still. Stand still.

Bounce will happen where I'm with you. I call it intercept. I'll intercept you. I gave you free will so that you could seek me on your own. That is more meaningful. You chose me, because you love me more than you love the things of this *world. Remember, we're no longer worried about how you'll get by. This isn't an exercise in optimism; it's an exercise in confidence in me.*

Begin With Silent Prayer

Give me peace, O, Lord, and help me to understand your way for me. Bring a calmness that opens me to an insight and helps me to understand what you're saying to me. Help me to comprehend my existence and why you created me. What am I meant to do in my life? Help me to find the energy to choose the paths you seek for me to take. O, Lord, I'm here to listen. I'm seeking to understand and thank you for being here with me. Amen.

Reflect—Use Your Imagination

As you complete the reading, put yourself into the Scripture. Imagine yourself as Saint Paul sitting in a room in Damascus, recovering from the terrible fall you had on the road that left you blind and confused. You were brought here to recover. After years of persecuting Christians, you were brought here to quietly listen to what the Lord wants of you. This is your wake-up call.

I don't understand my own actions. For I don't do what I want, but I do the very thing I hate. Now if I do what I don't want, I agree that the law is good. But in fact it is no longer I that do it, but sin that dwells within me. For I know that nothing good dwells within me, that is, in my flesh. I can will what is right, but I cannot do it. For I don't do the good I want, but the evil I don't want is what I do. Now if I do what I don't want, it is no longer I that do it, but sin that dwells within me.

So I find it to be a law that when I want to do what is good, evil lies close at hand. For I delight in the law of God in my inmost self, but I see in my members another law at war with the law of my mind, making me captive to the law of sin that dwells in my members.

Wretched man that I am! Who will rescue me from this body of death?

ROMANS 7:15–24

Saint Paul is identifying a challenge we all face—to live in reality, to cut through the layers of our false identity. Any of us can identify with Saint Paul's reference to sin as not living out the path for which we were created. Why do we choose those things that never seem to fully satisfy us? Why do we think one way and act another? Why do we set goals and not accomplish them? Why do we so often know what we should do and not do it? It relates to the fact that most of us are living as imposters. Who we are and what we were created to do is often in opposition to what we actually do.

Frequently our human frailties, our temptations, drive our actions. The person made fun of as a youth, to the point that weakness in his personality drove him to seek success throughout the rest of his life, only found failure. Today's reflection challenges us to get to the real truth of what we were meant to be. Understand that on this faith journey the true reflection of what we're meant to be will come through praise that is prayer, reverence that is appreciation, and service that is action in our lives related to our beliefs. If you're really going to get to the real core of who you're meant to be, the insights you receive will come from a depth of prayer, reverence, and service in the name of our Creator.

We live in a culture emphasizing goal orientation and achievement. Everything seems to be directed toward the seeking of this obscure idea of success, no matter what it means or what it costs. Acknowledging that we make choices in pure effort to achieve only success, our decisions often weaken our values, commitments, and the foundation of our beliefs. Accepting the fact that we were created to praise for prayer, to reverence God through humility, and to serve through our actions, our blindness will be stripped away and the motivations behind our superficial desires will be revealed. Eventually we'll have the ability to make choices from a pure desire of our hearts no longer guided by the world , but instead guided by Christ. We will discover the true meaning of success, and the fire in our hearts will ceaselessly burn for achievement of this success.

Engage Jesus in Conversation

Now that you've read the reflection and imagined yourself sitting in that dark room with Christ, write a brief answer to each of the questions. Realize that the answers are yours alone. Give yourself freedom to write whatever comes to mind. Let your mind go to the full feelings and understanding of where you are in terms of the question. At times you might write what you say to Jesus. At other times you'll find yourself writing what Jesus says to you. Be sure to date the conversation. If, while you're answering a question, another question comes to you, feel free to write it down. You'll find that over time, your ability to create your own questions will get you to a deeper level of reflection and conversation with the Lord.

- *Lord, what one thing can I do today that would serve you?*
- *How can I see you, O Lord, in my actions today?*
- *What gifts do I have that I can share with someone today?*
- *Who in my life brings me closer to you?*

Make Your Requests Known

Direct the questions you couldn't answer and any other questions that arose to Jesus, sitting there beside you. Ask him for insights into and confirmation of the thoughts you wrote down. Ask him to provide you with any additional reflections that will bring you to a deeper understanding of where you are in relationship to today's reflections.

Offer Thanks—Closing Prayer

Give thanks for this special time you shared in the presence of God. Ask him to give you the grace to observe and recognize his voice within you and his hand in your life, to see how Jesus is guiding you in the people with whom you connect.

Dear Lord, thank you for these great insights. There is nothing that I can do without you. Give me grace today to open my mind and heart to all you're sending to me. Help me to see in all that happens, in each experience you're speaking to me, calling my attention to what is happening to me and around me. Amen.

Evening Examen

Pause—Gain Interior Peace

Now is the time to find quiet away from the noise and confusion of the day. You're probably tired and may doze off. That's OK. Sit alone quietly. Concentrate on the voice within. Close your eyes for a few moments or focus your eyes on a single object for a brief time.

Enter—Practice the Presence—Face to Face

Place yourself in the presence of the Lord. Picture yourself sitting with Jesus. Think about how you yearn to understand what you experienced today. Imagine Jesus is speaking to you and listening to what you're saying. He offers no judgment, no tension. God in the person of Jesus Christ is sitting next to you in this very room.

Begin With Silent Prayer

O, Lord, please help me to understand today in my reflection the clarity of self, a decisiveness of purpose and an insight into why what I want to do or should do and what I choose to do are often in conflict. Come in to my heart and my mind in these next few minutes, break down the barriers of resistance, and open me to your message for me today. Amen.

Reflect—Use Your Imagination

Think about today. What happened that stood out in my mind?

- *If I felt frustration, where inside did it come from?*
- *If I experienced joy, what inside of me caused it?*
- *Each day brings both challenges and joys. Both bring us to insights about ourselves. Remember, you, like Paul, are on the road to Damascus, surprised by an encounter with the Lord, waking you up to the choices you've made in your life.*

Engage Jesus in Conversation

Living what we believe and doing what we were created to do is a lifelong journey.

As you reflect, imagine yourself sitting in a quiet room with Christ. Write a brief answer to each question. Realize that the answers are yours alone. Give yourself freedom to write whatever comes to mind. Let your mind go to the full feelings and understanding of where you are in terms of the question. At times, you might write what you say to Jesus. At other times, you'll find yourself writing what Jesus says to you. Be sure to date the conversation. If, while you're answering a question, another question comes to you, feel free to write it down. You'll find that over time, your ability to create your own questions will get you to a deeper level of reflection and conversation with the Lord.

- Lord, where did I miss the mark today ?

- Where today did my actions not follow my beliefs?

- Where today, Jesus, were you present in my life?

- How did my actions today show praise, reverence and service?

- What did I do today that brought me a single source of energy?

- How would my daily choices change if my life were based on faith-filled insights gained through prayer, humility and service?

- If I'm focused on seeking or achieving my eternal well-being, what would I have done differently today?

Make Your Requests Known

Now, share the answers you came up, with and the questions that you couldn't answer, with Jesus, sitting there with you. Ask him for insights and agreement to what you wrote down. Ask him to provide you with any additional reflections that will bring you to a deeper understanding of where you are in relationship to today's reflections.

O, Lord, am I asking the right questions? Where in my answers have I gone wrong? Am I finding clarity in what I think I should do, versus what I should do to better serve you? Where have I missed the mark? Help me see again.

Offer Thanks—Closing Prayer

Thank Jesus for special insights and grace He gave you this today.

Dear Lord, thank you for the special insights and grace of strength you gave me today. I already feel closer to you. I know that this is only the beginning. Help me each day to commit this time to you so that we can develop a deeper relationship. I want to live a life of purpose in your mission for me. There is nothing that I can do without you. Amen.

Second Encounter

See Yourself
As God Sees You

Morning Reflection

Pause—Gain Interior Peace

Be still. In the quiet, we hear God's voice. Separate yourself from thinking about all that you need to do today. Listen to the voice within. Close your eyes for a few moments or focus your eyes on a single object for a brief time.

Enter—Practice Dwelling in the Presence of Jesus—Face to Face

Place yourself in the presence of the Lord. You're sitting with Jesus. What a great opportunity! Think about how you yearn to understand yourself. Imagine Jesus is listening to what you're saying. He offers no judgment, no threat, and no tension. God in the person of Jesus Christ is sitting next to you in this very room.

He leans forward as he speaks to you...

Are you using the talents I gave you to do what you want or are you using them to do what I want? You've never taken the time to truly figure out what I wanted. You got close a couple of times. What you thought you needed to do to support your lifestyle took you away from me. I gave you insights. I gave you the ability to communicate those insights. I gave you the energy to go out to share those insights. I gave you the passion to get things done. You went away from the path I created for you because you wanted riches. You emulated those who confuse their lives with worldly riches.

I grew up in Nazareth in a family that was the poorest of the poor, but we understood why relationships were so important. I not asking you to be poor, and I'm certainly not asking you to stay busy. What I'm asking you is to listen to me. You talk virtue, you define your life in virtue, but you don't live you life in virtue. You have difficulty letting go of trying to be somebody, so that you can be my somebody. I'm saying that true joy comes when you quit projecting ourselves into everything that happens or everything that is said to you. For example, your need to be someone, your need to be acknowledged as important, creates resistance to the reality of my call for you. You missed it. But you still have time, even if it's only for a moment. Take a moment to tell me that you love me. Take a moment today to tell me that you realize it's not about you. Nothing is about you. Everything is about our relationship. Everything that you're called to do, everything you're gifted to do, is about our relationship. Do everything in my Father's name and everything will come to you in my Father's name! You operate with so much tension in your life because you want it your way.

Prepare then to turn it over to me.

Begin With Silent Prayer

Give me peace, O, Lord, and help me to understand your way for me. Bring calmness that brings me to an insight and helps me understand what you're saying to me. Help me understand why I exist and why you created me. Help me find energy and establish what paths you seek for me to take. O, Lord, I'm here to listen. Thank you for being here with me. Amen.

Reflect—Use Your Imagination

Place yourself in the situation you're reading about. Think of yourself at the moment God created you. Imagine yourself in Genesis when God created the world and everything he created was good. You're part of God's creation. You were part of his plan. You're in his plan.

So God created humankind in his image, in the image of God he created them; male and female he created them. God saw everything that he had made, and indeed, it was very good.

GENESIS 1:27–31

What a statement! God Almighty created us in his image and he found it good, He was pleased with it. When we think about that passage, why do so many of us disagree with the amazing message? We put ourselves down, seeing more wrong in ourselves than right.

Throughout any given day, even this day, the things we do right tend to blend into the woodwork. We focus on what we did wrong. We beat ourselves up, and somehow in the process we convince ourselves God is disappointed in us. We see ourselves through our own filter—not God's. While we think he sees us through a dark glass of guilt and condemnation, but he sees us only through the eyes of love.

Remember how unique each of us is. God threw away the mold when he created us. There is something unique about you that you bring to each day. Your uniqueness can affect the people around you in a positive way, and is, in essence, your journey to salvation. The key to experiencing that is to picture yourself as God sees you.

- *What aspects of us did he create that in turn signify the purpose in our lives?*
- *What talents and skills do we have?*
- *In short, how can each of us become clearer about our uniqueness in God's eyes?*
- *Each of us is invaluable to God.*

God understands we're human and that to be human is to fail. When we realize our gifts and understand their infinite value, we'll first and always understand that, in the midst of failure, we must challenge ourselves to stand up.

God created us and perfected us but gave us a human nature in which we also get confused from a lack of knowledge about ourselves and by permitting the world to influence us. Looking at the world, we try to decipher messages of affirmation and confirmation.

God bestowed within us a pure desire to seek him, not a desire to seek the things of the world in place of him. Being true to ourselves and recognizing ourselves as God sees us, we must look inside our own nature to identify the talents he gave us to serve him. So often, we use the gifts he gives us to accumulate things to satisfy ourselves rather than to serve him.

The truism in all of this is that to see ourselves as God sees us, we must focus on the unique qualities he created in us. The most joyful people with real, sustainable happiness realize they've been given a gift. Gifts not meant to be squandered—gifts freely given.

We also must understand there is nothing we can do to earn God's love. God loves us for who we are, not what we do. It's not our success as human beings that satisfies God; rather, it's contributing those gifts to activities, drawing God's glory into the experiences of every day life.

For example, if you have a gift of painting, paint so people can see the beauty in God's creation. Teach others that talent. The challenge for all of us is to see ourselves as servants in God's eyes, as partners in God's creation, rather than spending so much time focusing on what we do right or wrong. We need to focus on how we contribute our gifts in a communal way in order to exemplify the recognition of God's glory in the lives of people around us.

Make Your Requests Known

Now that you've read the reflection and imagined yourself in sitting in that dark room with Christ, write a brief answer to each of the questions. Realize that the answers are yours alone. Give yourself freedom to write whatever comes to mind. Let your mind go to the full feelings and understanding of where you are in terms of the questions. At times, you might write what you say to Jesus. At other times, you'll find yourself writing what Jesus says to you. Be sure to date the conversation. If you're answering a question and another question comes to you, feel free to write it down. You'll find that over time, your ability to create your own questions will get you to a deeper level of reflection and conversation with the Lord.

- *What unique skills and talents have you given me?*
- *How can I use them more effectively in my daily life to better serve you?*
- *Where can I be strong today and not be tempted by the possessiveness of the world?*

Engage Jesus in Conversation

Now, direct the questions that you couldn't answer, and the questions that you came up with on your own, to Jesus, sitting there with you. Ask him for insights and agreement to what you wrote down. Ask him to provide you with any additional reflections that will bring you to a deeper understanding of where you are in relationship to today's reflections.

Offer Thanks—Closing Prayer

Ask Jesus to be involved in your day. Ask him to give you guidance. Ask him to help you find insight to all you observe, recognizing where he is communicating with you. To see how Jesus is guiding you in the people with whom you connect.

O, Lord, please help me today to understand that I was created in your image and likeness. You infused talents and skills in me that draw me to serving you. The joy I bring to others through the skills and talents you give me are the tribute I give to you for being created. Come into my heart and mind today and clear away the desire of the things in this world that misdirect my efforts away from you and onto personal gratification. Thank you for this time together. Amen.

Evening Examen

Today gave you an opportunity to focus on your created uniqueness. Today gave you an opportunity to get closer to an understanding of what you have to offer to others. There is something God created especially for you.

Pause—Gain Interior Peace

It's time to be quiet. It's time to move away from all the stuff of today. As you sit quietly by yourself, listen to the voice within. Close your eyes for a few moments or focus your eyes on a single object for a brief time.

Enter—Practice Dwelling in the Presence of Jesus—Face to Face

Place yourself in the presence of the Lord. Imagine yourself sitting with Jesus. Think about how you yearn to understand what you experienced today. Each of us wants to understand what makes us different, what our unique gifts are, and how we're to use them. Imagine Jesus is speaking to you and listening to what you're saying. God in the person of Jesus Christ is sitting is with you, beside you in that very room.

Begin With Silent Prayer

O, Creator Father, please, help me to understand what happened to me today. Help me to understand the meaning of things that happened and didn't happen as I expected them to. In all of this, I'm seeking to see myself as you see me. What do you see in me that I should see and understand in myself?

As I begin my reflection, bring me clarity of self, a decisiveness of purpose, and an insight into where I missed the call today. Come into my heart and my mind in these next few minutes and break down the barriers of resistance. Open me to your message today. Amen.

Reflect—Use Your Imagination

Think about today.

- *What happened that stood out in my mind?*
- *If I was frustrated, what inside of me was the cause?*
- *If I experienced joy, what inside of me was the cause?*
- *Each day brings both challenges and joys. Both bring us insights about ourselves. Remember you, like Paul, are on the road to Damascus.*

Make Your Requests Known

Imagining yourself sitting in that quiet place with Christ, write a brief answer to each question. Realize that the answers are yours alone. Give yourself freedom to write whatever comes to mind. Let your mind go to the full feelings and understanding of where you are in terms of the question. At times, you might write what you say to Jesus. At other times, you'll find yourself writing what Jesus says to you. Be sure to date the conversation. If while you're answering that question, another question comes to you, feel free to write it down. You'll find that over time, your ability to create your own questions will get you to a deeper level of reflection and conversation with the Lord.

As part of your reflection, ask yourself these questions.

- *What today did I notice that was unique in me?*
- *What today did I do that was a gift to others?*
- *Where today did I find clarity in how God sees me?*
- *How today did my actions praise God?*
- *What today was the source of my energy?*

Engage Jesus in Conversation

Now, share the answers you came up with, and the questions that you couldn't answer, with Jesus, sitting there with you. Ask him for insights and agreement to what you wrote down. Ask him to provide you with any additional reflections that will bring you to a deeper understanding of where you are in relationship to today's reflections.

O, Lord, am I asking the right questions? Where in my answers have I gone wrong? Am I finding clarity in what I think I should do, vs. what I should do to better serve you? Where have I missed the mark?

Offer Thanks—Closing Prayer

Thank Jesus for special insights and grace he gave you today.

O, Lord, thank you for today and for the opportunity to gain insights into the uniqueness of me. Thank you for the clarity that I seek to achieve. Continue to help me better understand the value of my existence—what I have to bring to my family, my friends and my colleagues. I offer this and all my actions to your greater honor and glory. Amen.

Third Encounter

See God As God

Morning Reflection

Pause—Gain Interior Peace

As you quiet yourself, you move to hear God's voice. Separate yourself from thoughts regarding all you need to do today. Listen to the voice within you. Close your eyes for a few moments or focus your eyes on a single object for a brief time.

Enter—Practice Dwelling in the
Presence of Jesus—Face to Face

Place yourself in the presence of the Lord. You're sitting with Jesus. What a great opportunity. Think about your desire to understand yourself. Imagine Jesus is listening to what you're saying. He will offer no judgments and no negativity. God in the person of Jesus Christ is sitting next to you in this very room.

He leans forward as he speaks to you…

Listen to me carefully. This journey of discovery will change you, because it will bring you and me closer together, closer than we have ever been. You can open the door to me. I have been knocking for a long time and you were moving farther away from me. Just think! Twice a day with me isn't much, but it has already made a difference in you. So what do I want you to do? I want you to continue to stay with me, lunch with me, and block all the miscellaneous things out of your mind. Acknowledge only those things that come to you in faith, those things that come from me. Let's think of how we can make everything in your life converge with me.

This is about self-discovery, not about what you should be doing. You have no time! It's all my time, and right now, you need to be focused on our relationship of self-discovery. Then you'll hear me. Your life has come this way because you rarely live in the present and you're always worried about what is to come. In this time of reflection, you and I are one; you can hear me clearly in these moments, can't you? This is when you hear me inspiring you. It's not you that comes up with these responses; it's me working through you. You can do nothing without me. When you do my work, we're together. It flows. Let's continue to spend this time together. It will be OK. Everything with me is OK. Ask anyone who is close to me. Remember Martha and Mary. There is no rush. You have spent all these years rushing. If you died tomorrow, I wouldn't ask you what you got done. I would only ask you why you didn't spend more time with me.

Begin With Silent Prayer

O, Lord, I truly understand that as a mere human being, it's impossible for me to fully comprehend you as God; rather, I can come to know you as my creator. I can understand that you've given me certain unique gifts. Help me to understand that in my created nature there exists an opportunity for me to fulfill your purpose. Please help me to take the time to reflect on my purpose—to take time in my prayer to give you honor and glory. Help me to understand that in my very existence, I can know you as MY creator and MY Lord. You created me entirely unique—different from every other human or creature that also was created by your hand. I realize that as a human being, I can't fathom the omnipotence of you as God, but I can understand that there is a superior connection that draws you into my life. A connection, which challenges me to live a life that not only gives recognition to your existence, but truly works in the purpose for which you created me. Amen.

Reflect—Use Your Imagination

Place yourself in the situation into the Scripture. Imagine yourself at the moment God created you. Picture yourself in Genesis when God created the world and everything that he created was good. You're part of God's creation. You were a part of his plan. You're in his plan.

Hear, O Israel: The LORD is our God, the LORD alone. You shall love the LORD your God with all your heart, and with all your soul, and with all your might. Keep these words that I am commanding you today in your heart. Recite them to your children and talk about them when you are at home and when you are away, when you lie down and when you rise.

DEUTERONOMY 6:4–7

- *How do you see God?*
- *Do you see him as a holy but remote God-head type figure?*
- *Is your image of him as a grandfatherly, benevolent person we go running to when we're in trouble?*
- *Perhaps you see him as a no-nonsense, strict, unyielding dispenser of law and judgment?*

Each of us has a different view or image of him, much of it framed and designed by media, other believers, and literature. No doubt at some point we all have trouble getting our minds around who God is and how we view him. One thing is for certain: we all must realize that God is God and the being of God far exceeds any ability we have to see God as God. He reveals himself to us in many different and meaningful ways, but the question remains, how do we really see him in our own lives?

The challenge for us is to think of God as our creator—as the person who called us into being. He challenges us to seek through our creator a better understanding of ourselves and what we were created for. Struggling to attribute all that we have attained and all our gifts to our creator, we attempt to understand that in our created being there is an image and likeness that is attributable to

God. We were created for good and purpose; we were created to live a life that recognizes and acknowledges God as our creator and author. Our lives should naturally seek either positive or negative insight into purpose with everything that happens to us and in every opportunity. By giving honor to God, not just in prayer, but in our actions, we acknowledge the reality of our lives. The acknowledgement becomes our reality. In other words, prayer can't exist without a following action, because in the doing, we acknowledge God's existence to other people.

In the early days when people became catechumens and sought to enroll in this new Christian faith, they were drawn to it because they saw a uniqueness in the people who were Christian. Recognizing and acknowledging that these people understood something about God that they didn't understand, they witnessed a part of the way Christians lived their lives, which made their existence more real and more purposeful.

It's one thing to believe in God. It's another thing to acknowledge God in your life and beseech him to play an active role in your life, while you play an active role in acknowledging the existence of God through the outpouring of your actions. Our actions speak much more clearly than our "declarations" of faith. For example, I pray, but then I show anger to the person in the car next to me as I leave church. Or, I pray, but then I judge the actions of the foreign-born people at the table next to me at a restaurant. I say I believe in God, and I do believe in God, but can people see a difference in me that verifies my acknowledgement of the God who created me?

We struggle with four points in how we see God:

- We cannot understand God.
- We cannot understand that He created us.
- We can understand that in our lives, we have a responsibility to acknowledge the one who created us—God.
- We can live a life acknowledging that existence, and we can seek understanding by seeking God's intervention in our lives. We can draw on what he created us for and whatever gifts he created within us, in order to serve in his stead for the betterment of other people. We can stretch ourselves to live and serve, not just for the betterment of people as they go about the business of living, but to impact them in their acknowledgement that they are created beings and there is a God in their lives.

My service can't just be helping the poor—it must be helping the poor in the light of the purpose that comes from my existence given to me by God.

Make Your Requests Known

Now that you have read the reflection and imagined yourself in sitting in that dark room with Christ, write a brief answer to each question. Realize that the answers are yours alone. Give yourself freedom to write whatever comes to mind. Let your mind go to the full feelings and understanding of where you are in terms of the question. At times you might write what you say to Jesus. At other times you'll find yourself writing what Jesus says to you. Be sure to date the conversation. If while you're answering that question, another question comes to you, feel free to write it down. Over time, your ability to create your own questions will move you to a deeper level of reflection and conversation with the Lord.

- *Today, how can I acknowledge, not only through prayer but through actions, that I'm your created son (daughter)?*
- *How can I look into the face and heart of others and see the uniqueness that you created in them?*
- *What do I face today in the challenges of my life that will keep me from living out the recognition of you as God and creator?*

Engage Jesus in Conversation

Now, direct the questions that you couldn't answer and the questions that you came up with on your own, to Jesus, sitting there with you. Ask him for insights and agreement to what you wrote down. Ask him for clarity. Ask him to help create a seamless connection between your prayer life and your action life—your doing. Ask him how to use your talents to acknowledge him. Ask him how to be more than just a nice person. Ask him to help you dig deeply into the activities of this day and acknowledge whatever the outcomes. Ask him to help you do all things in his honor and glory and in appreciation for having created you.

Offer Thanks—Closing Prayer

Ask Jesus to be involved with you to day. Ask him to give you guidance. Ask him to help you listen when he is talking to you. To recognize in the experiences you have today, how he is speaking to you. To see in the people you connect with how Jesus is guiding you.

> O, Lord, I so much appreciate all you do for me each day. I understand that I'll never be satisfied in this earthly environment, but each day, I'll increase my acknowledgement of your role in my life. Help me today to pause and to find in the silence, a way to reflect on the true value and importance of my life as one aimed to acknowledge your existence and effect on me. Amen.

Evening Examen

Today, God gave you great opportunities. He gave you opportunities to see him in the face and hearts of those around you. To see God through Jesus Christ you must look for God around you, in the things he created, in the people he sends into your life, in the situations that he draws you into. Seeing God as God calls us to look for him. We must realize that as we look for God we come to realize that he is inside of us. We're created in his image and likeness. Unfortunately, because of the routine of our existence, the images of God quickly fade into the background.

Pause—Gain Interior Peace

It's time to quiet yourself again. It's time to move away from all the stuff of today, away from the tension of the day. As you sit quietly by yourself, open yourself to listen to the voice within. Close your eyes for a few moments or focus your eyes on a single object for a few moments

Enter—Practice the Presence—Face to Face

Place yourself in the presence of the Lord. Imagine you're sitting with Jesus. Think about how you yearn to understand what you experienced today, how you desire to see the Lord as part of your daily encounters. Each of us wants to understand where the Lord is active in our lives. Each of us wants to know that we aren't alone on our journey. Over time, we become sensitive to the presence of the Lord. God in the person of Jesus Christ is sitting with you, beside you, now.

Begin With Silent Prayer

O, Lord, please help me to understand what happened to me today. Help me to understand the meaning of things that happened and didn't happen as I expected them to. In all of this, I'm seeking to see you as God. I know that you're with me. I know that you care about me and all that happens to me. Help me to see you in all I encounter. As I begin this reflection bring me clarity, a decisiveness of purpose, and an insight into where I missed your presence today. Come into my heart and my mind in these next few minutes and break down the barriers of confusion. Open me to your message for me today. Amen.

Reflect—Use Your Imagination

Think about today, the people you met, the things that you experienced. Ask yourself these questions:

- *What happened today that stood out in my mind?*
- *Where did I see the Lord today?*
- *What did he share with me today in the things that happened to me?*
- *If I experienced joy, what was the cause?*

Each day bring both challenges and joys. Both bring us insights into the presence of the Lord. Remember the Lord is with you always. It's coming to recognize his hand in your life that guides you to understand what he is calling you to do with your life.

Make Your Requests Known

Now write a brief answer to each of the following questions. Realize that the answers are yours alone. Give yourself freedom to write whatever comes to mind. Let your mind go to the full feelings and understanding of where you are in terms of the question. At times you might write what you say to Jesus. At other times you'll find yourself writing what Jesus says to you. Be sure to date the conversation. If, while you're answering a question, another question comes to you, write it down. You'll find that over time, your ability to create your own questions will get you to a deeper level of reflection and conversation with the Lord.

As part of your reflection, ask yourself these questions.

- *Where today did I look a little deeper into the face of others to see God?*
- *How did my actions reflect my beliefs in God as God?*
- *How today did I acknowledge God as my creator?*
- *What actions today praised God?*

Engage Jesus in Conversation

Now, share the answers you came up with and the questions that you couldn't answer with Jesus, sitting there with you. Read them out loud if you can. Ask him for insights and agreement to what you wrote down. Ask him to provide you with any additional reflections that will bring you to a deeper understanding of where you are in relationship to today's reflections.

O, Lord, am I asking the right questions? Where in my answers have I missed your message? Am I finding clarity in what you're saying to me? What I should do recognize your presence in whom I meet and what I experience?

Offer Thanks—Closing Prayer

Thank Jesus for the special insights and grace He gave you this day.

O, Lord, thank you for today and for the opportunity to gain insights into where you were present in my day. Thank you for the clarity that I seek to understand in your working in my day. Continue to help me better understand what you're calling me to do. I offer this and all my actions to your greater honor and glory. Amen.

Fourth Encounter

Focus on Eternal Well-Being

Morning Reflection

Pause—Gain Interior Peace

As you quiet yourself, you move to hear God's voice. Separate yourself from thinking about all that you need to do today. Listen to the voice within. Close your eyes for a few moments or focus your eyes on a single object for a brief time.

Enter—Practice Dwelling in the
Presence of Jesus—Face to Face

Place yourself in the presence of the Lord. You're sitting with Jesus. What a great opportunity! Think about how you yearn to understand yourself, how you yearn for joy and purpose in your life. Total fulfillment in *this* life isn't possible, but the joy of knowing you're preparing yourself for paradise, that you're focusing on your eternal well-being, brings you a sense of joy and fulfillment. Imagine Jesus is listening to what you're saying. He offers no judgment and no tension. God in the person of Jesus Christ is sitting next to you in that very room.

He leans forward as he speaks to you…

You're getting closer to me. I'm the only point of view. Just as in Mark's Gospel, "Rising, I got up early before dawn and went to a deserted place to pray with my Father," you're taking this time to pray with me and the Father. You have spent your life filling your days with activities that were disconnected from me. It's one thing to offer your day up to me. It's another thing to live that day from my point of view. That's why your life was so complicated. Focusing on me simplifies all things. There is a common denominator that brings unity (**unum necessarium**), what you seek to discover. In the Gospel as reported by Luke (14:18–20), you must place everything in direct relationship with me and your questions will be answered. When you seek the highest value and the deepest good, everything gets simpler.

The world offers you a gifted person, who focuses her attention on many different things. In the midst of working on everything, she still finds herself empty and longing. Although she is busy, she feels nothing she does fulfills her. Then it becomes "many" at the expense of much. You think the more things you get done the better off you'll be. Your eternal well-being comes from focusing on much that is doing one thing well. That is doing the thing I have called you to do well. At times, you're very impatient. Remember as I have told you before, it's not what you do in your life, but your relationship with me that gives meaning to what you do in life.

As you continue to understand yourself and seek a deeper real relationship with me, you'll find the things you need to do become more obvious. Listen to what you say to yourself and others. Your dialogue should bring the light of truth to all you *encounter. When you define what you should be doing from my point of view, that will change in your focus. Then you'll get the idea of what I want you to be. You got close to it by listening to your heart's desires. Here's a hint: be a person of God, serve the Lord, bring God's purpose to everything you do, help others discover God's presence in their lives, live the Scriptures— make straight the way of the Lord.*

Begin With Silent Prayer

O, Heavenly Father, help me to understand today that it's not in the quality of my life but the commitment of my life that I'll find joy and eternal well-being. Help me to see how I can more fully live out my call by getting into what I'm doing. Help me realize that merely changing jobs or friends or roles in life doesn't bring a greater opportunity to give you tribute. It's in where I'm at in this moment and how I deal with being in that place that I can more fully use the gifts I have to draw me to the opportunities that will allow me to truly fulfill your purpose. Amen.

Reflect—Use Your Imagination

Place yourself in the situation that you're reading. Put yourself into the Scripture. Think of your eternal well-being, think of paradise. Picture yourself in Genesis in the Garden of Eden before Adam's fall, when life had no tension, when life was purely praising God. You're part of God's creation. You were part of his plan. You're in his plan.

> *My brothers and sisters, whenever you face trials of any kind, consider it nothing but joy, because you know that the testing of your faith produces endurance; and let endurance have its full effect, so that you may be mature and complete, lacking in nothing.*
>
> *If any of you is lacking in wisdom, ask God, who gives to all generously and ungrudgingly, and it will be given you. But ask in faith, never doubting, for the one who doubts is like a wave of the sea, driven and tossed by the wind.*

JAMES 1:2–6

Truly, everything that God has created is good and has purpose. We get confused when we see darkness and evil. We wonder how could God permit that, or did God create that terrible hurricane or earthquake? Yet everything in the world is to help us focus on our eternal well-being. This concept is foreign to our minds. Conformed to the world's image, we believe we must do anything and everything possible to keep anything bad or uncomfortable or sad out of our lives or from touching any of our loved ones. Of course, no one wants bad things to happen to them. At the same time, God can use good and bad to promote our well-being.

It's not a matter of thinking that only good things are worthy. If something helps us, good or bad, we should use it. If it hinders us we should stay away from it. God created all things and all things are initially good—it's the misuse of God's creation that causes sin and suffering.

The fundamental challenge for us isn't to think about the individual things we have on any given day, but to focus our eyes on the goal of life and our ultimate end—our salvation. When we put it in terms of that ultimate eternal well-being, we discover unlimited opportunities in the created things of this world. From that perspective, we can then understand that we should use any part of our lives that could potentially lead us to salvation, thus, avoiding those things that hinder it. If they don't purely contribute to our salvation, we should avoid them as well. Candy is good, but gorging ourselves on it won't benefit us in any way. Good is good, bad is bad—it's our use of good or bad that leads us to God and his mission for us.

The objective here is that whether we're wealthy or poor, there is no excuse not to get to heaven. Heaven has its doors open to all. We all have different jobs and lives. Some of us love our jobs and lives and some of us hate our jobs and lives. Whether we love them or hate them, our jobs and lives carry us along the path to God's purpose.

It matters little to God which job we have, but there is a huge difference in how we use that job to manifest his will for our lives. There is a tendency to believe that our ability to be a "good person" is anchored in our jobs, lives, and measures of success.

We have a vocation that goes beyond the tasks we do to procure a paycheck. For example, I've always believed that there is ministry in administration. There is a great pastoral role in being an administrator, a mother, or a father. Your job may be to manage an office or a family of seven, but your vocation is to show the love and grace of God to all those you touch through that job.

Mountain climbers have a philosophy that says, "If you can't get out of it—then get into it." If you're halfway up the side of a cliff, and you can't get down, then go up. The cliff won't change, but you do. Even if you don't have the perfect job, relationship, kids, or friends, you have wonderful opportunities each day to live out your purpose through them. If you have a job or a situation you don't like, make up your mind to be the best at it you can. By being the best at something, even something that isn't your choice for yourself, there is an opportunity to hone in on the purpose of your life. In that challenge, you can learn the most. In those dark times or situations, the only real source of strength is prayer. Prayer in and of itself isn't the answer. Prayer doesn't turn all bad to good. Prayer is the strength that brings us to the answer and our source for life—God's purpose.

Make Your Requests Known

Now that you've read the reflection and imagine yourself in the Garden of Eden with Christ, write a brief answer to each question. Realize that the answers are yours alone. Give yourself freedom to write whatever comes to mind. Let your mind go to the full feelings and understanding of where you are in terms of the question. At times you might write what you say to Jesus. At other times you'll find yourself writing what Jesus says to you. Be sure to date the conversation. If, while you're answering that question, another question comes to you, feel free to write it down. You'll find that over time, your ability to create your own questions will get you to a deeper level of reflection and conversation with the Lord.

- *Lord, what one thing can I do today in the midst of my current job and relationships that will be an opportunity to serve you and serve my life's purpose?*
- *How today can I take each opportunity and fulfill it to the ultimate, knowing that you'll guide me to where you want me to be in my life.*

Engage Jesus in Conversation

Now, direct the questions that you couldn't answer, and the questions that you came up with on your own, to Jesus, sitting there with you in the garden. Ask him for insights and agreement to what you wrote down. Ask him for clarity. Ask him to help create a seamless connection between your prayer life and your action life—your doing. Ask him how to use your talents to acknowledge him as God. Ask him how to be more than just a nice person. Ask him to help you dig deeply into the activities of this day and acknowledge whatever the outcomes. Do all things in his honor and glory and in appreciation for having created you.

Offer Thanks—Closing Prayer

Ask Jesus to be involved in your day. Ask him to give you guidance. Ask him to help you see within, where he is talking to you, in the experiences you have today, to understand how he is speaking to you. To see in the people you connect with how Jesus is guiding you.

Dear Lord, thank you for keeping me close to you. Thank you for the graces and the insights that you make available to me. Please help me to pause when I need to pause, so that I may understand the opportunities before me, even if the situations that I find myself in today aren't totally what I thought they would be. I seek to follow your call on earth in what I do today. I seek to give greater honor and glory to you. Amen.

Evening Examen

Today gave you an opportunity to focus on the fact that everything in your life isn't perfect. Only God is perfect. Understanding God as God brings you closer to fulfilling his purpose for your life. Everything you encountered today in the world affords an opportunity for you to gain an understanding of how everything works to bring us closer to the comprehension of God's purpose for us. We weren't a mistake. We were created for a purpose. He created us to fulfill his mission on earth. There will be different paths for all of us on the way to that mission.

Pause—Gain Interior Peace

In spite of the rigors of your day, it's time to quiet yourself again. It's time to move away from all the stuff, away from the tension. This is special time. Don't worry about taking this time to reflect. As you sit quietly by yourself, open yourself to listen to the voice within. Close your eyes for a few moments or focus your eyes on a single object for a few moments.

Enter—Practice the Presence—Face to Face

Place yourself in the presence of the Lord. Think about sitting with Jesus. Think about how much he knows about you. Think about all the insights he has about your day. Today, God was very active in your life. Each of us wants to understand where the Lord speaks to us, and what he is saying. These past days you have become sensitive to the presence of the Lord.

Begin With a Prayer

O, Lord, today was a special day. Please help me to understand what insights I gained today and how they relate to my eternal well-being. Help me to understand the meaning of things that happened and didn't happen as I expected them to. In all of this, I seek to understand what it's that I do that gives honor and glory to you. I know that you're with me. I know that you care about me and are leading me to eternity with you. But the world is so confusing. At times, I don't see how my faith fits into my activities. Help me understand what I should have done differently. Help me to see you in all I encounter. As I begin this reflection, bring me clarity and a decisiveness of purpose. Come into my heart and my mind in these next few minutes and break down the barriers of confusion, and open me to your message for me today. Amen.

Reflect—Use Your Imagination

Think about the people you met and the things that you experienced today. Each day brings both challenges and joys. Both bring you insights into the presence of the Lord. Both give you insights into how you should focus your efforts toward your eternal well-being. Remember, the Lord is with you always. You're coming to recognize his hand in your life guiding you to understand what he is calling you to do with your life. Ask yourself these questions:

- *What happened today that stood out in my mind?*
- *Where did I see the Lord today?*
- *What did he share with me today in the things that happened to me?*
- *When I experienced joy, what was the cause?*

Make Your Requests Known

Now write a brief answer to each of the following questions. Realize that the answers could be similar to those from a previous day, because you're getting clearer in your relationship with Jesus. Give yourself freedom to write whatever comes to mind. Let your mind go to the full feelings and understanding of where you are in terms of the question. At times, you might write what you say to Jesus. You're noticing that more of your answers are coming from Jesus and fewer from you. Date the conversation. If while you're writing, another question comes to you, write it down. You have found that your own questions will get you to a deeper level of reflection and conversation with the Lord.

As part of your reflection, ask Jesus these questions.

- *Where today did I see an opportunity to gain more understanding of what I need to do in my life to serve God more fully?*
- *Where today did I complain that my opportunities didn't fit me properly?*
- *Where today did I brush a person aside because I thought he or she wasn't important in my day?*
- *What did I do today to "get into it" rather than try to "get out of it"?*
- *What today was the source of my energy?*

Engage Jesus in Conversation

Now, share your answers with Jesus. Read them out loud if you can. Ask him agreement to what you wrote down. At times, he will disagree and give you additional insights that will bring you to a deeper understanding of where you are in relationship to today's experiences.

O, Lord, am I asking the right questions? Where in my answers have I missed your message? Am I finding clarity in what you're saying to me? What I should do recognize your presence in who I meet and what I experience?

Offer Thanks—Closing Prayer

Thank Jesus for special insights and grace He gave you this today.

O, Lord, thank you for all the grace you gave me today. Without you, I can do nothing and with you, I can focus on my eternal well-being, heaven. Thank you for the insights I have gained during this reflection. Thank you for the clarity that I seek to understand where my work was your work this day. I know that you'll continue to help me better understand what you're calling me to do. I offer this and all my actions to your greater honor and glory. Amen.

Fifth Encounter

See the World As God Does

Morning Reflection

Pause—Gain Interior Peace

Move to quiet yourself to hear his voice. Some days, this is more difficult than others. If it takes slightly more time today, that's all right; Jesus isn't in a hurry. You have the rest of your life. Separate yourself from thinking about all that you need to do today. Listen to the voice within. Find an object that brings attention to a sharp focus. Use a tree or a bird. Remember God created everything to remind us of him.

Enter—Practice Dwelling in the
Presence of Jesus—Face to Face

Focus on his presence. Realize that you might not feel him there with you at first, but he is there. As you reflect with him, you're coming to know he is always there. He is bringing you joy as you come to see your purpose in this world. Total fulfillment in this life, as you know, isn't possible, but the world is providing you with the tools to prepare yourself for paradise. If you see the world as God sees it, you'll come to use it as the way to salvation. What you do in the world with those you encounter and the circumstances you experience are all part of your journey. Jesus is listening. He offers insights and encouragement, not judgment. Jesus wants you to understand how God the Father sees the world.

He leans forward as he speaks to you…

Your world gets confusing. My Father made it a paradise, but with freewill. Adam sought to use it for his purpose; he sought to make it his object, not mine. In so doing, he turned it into a place that challenges you, tempts you, and leads you away from me. It's a world where pain is part of life. It's a world where people take advantage of others to get more of what they want. Life becomes about work. Life becomes about having things. Life becomes about anything but me. At times, you think that you must separate your faith from your work. You don't think that I fit into the world. I'm the world; why would I not fit into it?

You worry too much about all you have to do in the world. You worry about all you're not getting done. I'm not asking you to give up what you're doing. I'm asking you to do it with me as the object of that action. For that to happen, for you to do your work with me in mind, we need to get closer so that we can share like this throughout the day, not just these few minutes in the morning. You keep wondering if this time is worth it. All time you spend with me is worth it. But it must come to action. Remember, "a tree is known by its fruit" (Luke 6:44). You're known by your actions.

As we continue to spend this time together, you'll come to make me part of you day. You'll put your confidence in me so that you can deal with the world, so that you can live your faith in your daily life. You have tried to put confidence in yourself; that's optimism. On your own, optimism won't last. What you need is confidence in me that will support your optimism. You're beginning to understand that working on our relationship will bring you some real insight. This needs to be a routine for the

> rest of your life of transformation. I know that you hate routine,
> but it was never satisfying before. You have always lived under
> fear and ego anxiety. Bring me yourself in love, and I'll direct
> your day. Quit trying to accomplish things that I don't intend
> for you to accomplish. Remember, transformation only comes
> through your relationship with me. Everything was created for a
> purpose. That is a higher purpose. Relax and let it come to you
> through me.

Begin With Silent Prayer

*O, Lord, help me today to understand the many ways I'm con-
fused about my purpose. I find myself seeking the things of this
world to satisfy some need I have, and in the midst of gaining
those things, I have failed to see the needs in others. Lord, I
realize that in the needs of others is the very purpose to which
I'm called. Come into my mind and heart today. Help me to
clear the haze from my eyes and make me sensitive to the needs
of those around me so that I can recognize my Lazarus. Amen.*

Reflect—Use Your Imagination

Place yourself in the situation that you're about to read. Put yourself into the Scripture. Imagine how God sees the world. Picture
yourself at the table with the rich man who is ignoring Lazarus.
Think of being in God's world but having free choice to do what
you want or what God wants of you.

There was a rich man who was dressed in purple and fine linen and who feasted sumptuously every day. And at his gate lay a poor man named Lazarus, covered with sores, who longed to satisfy his hunger with what fell from the rich man's table; even the dogs would come and lick his sores. The poor man died and was carried away by the angels to be with Abraham. The rich man also died and was buried. In Hades, where he was being tormented, he looked up and saw Abraham far away with Lazarus by his side. He called out, "Father Abraham, have mercy on me, and send Lazarus to dip the tip of his finger in water and cool my tongue; for I am in agony in these flames." But Abraham said, "Child, remember that during your lifetime you received your good things, and Lazarus in like manner evil things; but now he is comforted here, and you are in agony."

LUKE 16:19–25

The differences between people and the opportunities we have is that we all use them differently. Some take advantage and use them to gain power over other people, to oppress, or in some cases, destroy. Yet, there are those who use their God-given opportunities to benefit those who don't have the same advantages. Instead of breaking others down, they lift people up.

God sees all of us in our nakedness. He doesn't see our houses or cars. He doesn't know us by the letters after our names, designating some measure of success or ability. He doesn't know us by our jobs. Instead he knows us by how we use our gifts, possessions, and advantages to benefit our journey and purpose in life.

The story of Lazarus and the Rich Man helps each of us get a clear picture of who we're and how we react to others.

- *Are you the rich man?*
- *Are you the one with all the possessions—the one who passes by people in need?*
- *Are you the one using possessions with the goal of merely acquiring more?*

Possessions themselves aren't bad. Fame, fortune, recognition aren't bad, but any of these used for something other than achieving our eternal well-being is misused.

Take a moment and imagine yourself as the rich man who sees Lazarus at his gate day after day. Then think of yourself as Lazarus, who sees the rich man pass him by again and again.

Think of how you would feel as Lazarus. Knowing that, for whatever reason, your path in life doesn't equal that of the rich man. Your opportunities haven't worked out to make you rich in material things. Yet, the Lazaruses of this world often see things the rich man doesn't. They have a sense about life and purpose that can only come from seeing their world clearly. Those of us who, for whatever reasons, have been able to accumulate wealth and possessions are often blinded by those very same possessions to what our real purpose and calling in life is.

Put yourself in the rich man's place and think about who might be the Lazarus in your life. Who has reached out to you for help, perhaps asked you for understanding and you passed them by? How many Lazaruses are there around you?

The question begs to be asked, why have you missed seeing them—are there so many possessions between you and the Lazarus in your life that you fail to see what may be right in front of you?

People who jump in their cars, head to the lake for the weekend, stay on the go every minute, and then come back to work, only to jump on the treadmill again, making money to buy more things, are truly the ones with blinded eyes. In the blinding drive to just accumulate more, they fail to see the purpose in life.

Today, let's spend a moment trying to recognize the Lazarus in our lives by putting ourselves in his place. Purpose in life doesn't come through acquiring things but through the realization of the application of the gifts we have received to fulfill our purpose.

Make Your Requests Known

Write a brief answer to each question. Realize that the answers are yours alone. Give yourself freedom to write whatever comes to mind about the world, about Lazarus, or the rich man. Let your mind go to the full feelings and understanding of where you are in terms of the question. At times you're writing what you say to Jesus. At other times, you'll write what Jesus says to you. Be sure to date the conversation. If another question comes to you, write it down. Over time, your ability to create your own questions will get you to a deeper level of reflection and conversation with the Lord.

Imagine what it's like for God to see you in this world.

- *Lord, as I carry out my daily actions what do you see in me?*
- *Then imagine what it would be like to be Lazarus—with nothing. No opportunities, possessions, or fame.*
- *How will my choices today be different?*
- *What insights will I gain?*
- *What will I do today because someone in my world calls for help?*
- *What can I do today that will give my life more meaning?*

Engage Jesus in Conversation

Now, direct the questions that you couldn't answer and the questions that you came up with on your own, to Jesus, sitting there with you. Ask him for insights into what you wrote down. Ask him for clarity. Ask him to help you see the world as he does. Ask him how to use your gifts to help those around you today. Ask him to help you dig deeply into the activities of this day and acknowledge that whatever the outcomes are, you'll do all things in his honor and glory and in appreciation for what he has given you to pass on to others.

Offer Thanks—Closing Prayer

Ask Jesus to be involved in your day. Ask him to give you guidance. Ask him to help you see within all you observe, where he is asking you to help Lazarus. Ask him to help you understand in the experiences you have today how he is reaching out to you. To see in the people you connect with how Jesus is guiding you.

Dear Lord, thank you for the insights during this reflection. There are so many things I'm coming to realize about myself and my purpose and how I've lived my life. Help me today to continue to close the gap between what I want and what you want, between what I believe and what you know. Between the actions that I take based upon my desires and the actions I should take based upon your desires. I see the world differently. It's a place where I'm called to give of what you've given me. I offer you this day all my actions and thoughts for your greater honor and glory. Amen.

Evening Examen

Today you're gaining insights into the reality of your purpose. The actions you take each day towards that purpose will further your ability to distance yourself from your need for material goods. Today's example helped you understand the rich man's attitude toward Lazarus and the attitude of Lazarus toward the rich man. Today we have sought to gain more insights into what it's like to see a world that passes you by.

Pause—Gain Interior Peace

In spite of the rigors of your day it's time to quiet yourself again. It's time to move away from all the stuff, away from the tension. This is special time to still yourself, in order to get a clearer understanding of where Jesus was coming to you. As you sit quietly by yourself, open yourself to listen to the voice within. Feel free to close your eyes for a few moments or focus your eyes on a single object for a brief time.

Enter—Practice the Presence—Face to Face

Jesus is present with you. Place yourself in his presence. Think about him sitting there beside you. Think about how much he knows about you, think about all the insights he has about how your day has been. Today, he was very active in your life. Each of us wants to understand where the Lord speaks to us, and what he is saying. Each day, you become more sensitive to his presence.

Begin With a Prayer

O, Lord, today was a special day. Help me to understand why I have difficulty detaching myself from worldly things. Give me insights as to where I could have reached out to those around me, like Lazarus. Help me to understand the meaning of things that happened and didn't happen as I expected them to. In all of this, I seek to understand what it's that I do that gives honor and glory to you through those around me. I know that you're with me. I know that you care about me and are leading me to serve in your name, but my world seems so demanding. It's hard to find time to stop and help those who seem to be in need. Help me understand what I should have done differently. Help me to see you in all I encounter. As I begin this reflection, bring me clarity and a decisiveness of purpose. Come into my heart and my mind in these next few minutes and break down the barriers of confusion and open me to your message for me today. Amen.

Reflect—Use Your Imagination

Think about the people you met and the things that you experienced today. Each day brings both challenges and joys. Both bring you insights into the presence of the Lord. Both give you insights into where you should focus your efforts toward serving others in the name of the Lord. Remember, the Lord is with you always. You're coming to recognize his hand in your life that guides you to understand what he is calling you to do with your life. Ask yourself these questions:

- *What happened today that stood out in my mind?*
- *Where did I encounter someone who reminds me of Lazarus?*
- *What could I have done that I didn't do?*

Make Your Requests Known

Now write a brief answer to each of the following questions. Realize that the answers could be similar to those from a previous day. This happens because you're getting clearer in your relationship with Jesus. Give yourself freedom to write whatever comes to mind. Let your mind go to the full feelings and understanding of where you are in terms of the question. You're noticing that more of your answers are coming from Jesus and fewer from you. Date the conversation. If while you're writing, another question comes to you, write it down. You have found that your own questions will get you to a deeper level of reflection and conversation with the Lord.

As part of your reflection, ask Jesus these questions:

- *Lord, where today did I miss an opportunity to serve a Lazarus?*
- *What did I learn about the world as God sees it?*
- *Where was God's clarity present in my life today?*
- *How did my actions today show a lack of attachment to worldly things and a better understanding of the needs of Lazarus?*
- *What was the source of my energy today?*

Engage Jesus in Conversation

Now, share your answers with Jesus. Read them out loud if you can. Ask him for agreement to what you wrote down. At times, he will gently disagree and give you additional insights that will bring you to a deeper understanding of where you are in relationship to today's experiences.

O, Lord, am I asking the right questions? Where in my answers have I missed your message? Am I finding clarity in what you're saying to me? What I should do recognize your presence in whom I meet and what I experience?

Offer Thanks—Closing Prayer

Thank Jesus for the special insights and grace he gave you today.

O, Lord, thank you for all the grace you gave me today. Without you, I can do nothing, and with you, I can focus on serving others in your name. Thank you for the insights I have gained during this reflection. Thank you for the clarity that I seek to understand where my work was your work this day. Thank you for opening my eyes to those around me who need help in their lives. I know that you'll continue to help me better understand what you're calling me to do. I offer this and all my actions to your greater honor and glory. Amen.

Sixth Encounter

See People As Jesus Does

Morning Reflection

Pause—Gain Interior Peace

Move to quiet yourself in order to hear his voice. This is becoming easier each day. Remember, Jesus isn't in a hurry. He isn't going to rush off on you. You have the rest of your life. Separate yourself from thinking about all that you need to do today. Listen to the voice within. Find an object that gets your attention and try to focus on it briefly or simply close your eyes and peer into the nothingness of your vision.

Enter—Practice Dwelling in the
Presence of Jesus—Face to Face

Focus on his presence. Realize at times you might not feel him there with you, but he is there. He is always there. You're coming to know that as you reflect with him. You have been getting clearer insights into things that happen to you. He is bringing you joy as you come to see your purpose in this world. Total fulfillment in this life isn't possible. but every day you're provided with the tools to develop a deeper relationship with Jesus. Sometimes, it's a person; at other times, it's a situation. It might even be a desire that he places in your heart that will serve his Father's purpose on earth. If you see people the way that Jesus does, you'll come to realize his presence in all you meet. You'll come to see how they participate in the purpose for which you were created. What you do in the world with those you encounter is part of your journey. Jesus is listening. He offers insights into those you'll encounter this day. Jesus wants you to understand how he sees the meaning of people in your life.

He leans forward as he speaks to you...

The time you're spending with me is serious. This is more serious than anything else you have to do. Since you've started coming to me in this way, your life is better. Less fear? Less tension? Not as much as you expected? You can't expect immediate change after a life of doing what you wanted. You're discovering transformation. Transformation can only come through me. I'm transforming you.

No longer will optimism be your definition for life, as it has been in the past. Now it's confidence in me that will be the foundation of your life. Bring everything to me. Ask me. Listen to me. Then you'll come to know what is really important. I send special people into your life each day to confirm my journey; some you already know and take for granted, and some are new. You don't recognize me in them. Remember, these reflections are only small steps, but they bring us together for the rest of your life; then you'll join me forever.

Life with me is simple; life without me is a challenge. As we walk and talk and work together, we're praying to my Father together. As we go forward, we'll cry together. When it's all done, the fulfillment that you'll have is in the intimacy of your relationship with me. There will be eternal life with me.

You're still experiencing some despair. You're impatient with a journey that has no deadline, no list of things to do, only one demand and that is to spend time with me. If you really want things to change, you'll have to continue to get out of your boat and really get to know people around you. You'll be transformed through me and those I send into your life.

Everyone you encounter has a purpose under heaven!

Begin With Silent Prayer

O, God, I truly understand that it's not how I see myself at this point, but how I see you. In that, I'll come to understand the true purpose in my life. I also understand that often in coming to understand you, I'll understand myself and others better. I'll come to understand more clearly the people you've brought into my life. They are also your gifts to me. Show me how to relate to them, so that I can come to know your will for me. It's not my purpose, but yours, that I seek. Please help me today to better understand my purpose. In the embrace of those around me, you're seeking to help me understand something I don't understand and something I need to prepare myself for your service. Amen.

Reflect—Use Your Imagination

Place yourself in the situation that you're about to read. Put yourself into the Scripture. Think about how Jesus sees people. Imagine yourself as someone who observes Christ encounter the blind man. Think of the works of God that are displayed through the blind man.

As he walked along, he saw a man blind from birth. His disciples asked him, 'Rabbi, who sinned, this man or his parents, that he was born blind?' Jesus answered, 'Neither this man nor his parents sinned; he was born blind so that God's works might be revealed in him.'

JOHN 9:1–3

Throughout Scripture, we observe that Jesus didn't judge people based upon who they were or where they were from. He sought more to understand them as human beings created by his Father.

In all things he looked to what people did rather than who they were. He chastised the Scribes and Pharisees for accusing him of breaking the law by healing a man's withered hand on the Sabbath. They were more concerned about the law than showing compassion and kindness. No doubt, they were quite proud of their standing in life and how spiritual they were; yet, Jesus was concerned with healing someone—giving a gift of life. Jesus didn't care who they were; rather he cared about what they did or didn't do.

Yes, Jesus sees our hearts, not our occupations or how many letters we have behind our name. He sees our motives and our nature. Does that mean that only "bad people" suffer? We know that isn't true! Everyone suffers at some point in life. Yet, many of us think that when we suffer it's punishment from God for something we have done.

As we see in the Scripture for today, Jesus taught his disciples that the blindness of the man wasn't a result of his deeds or those of his parents. Jesus used what was tragic to display what God could do through him. Jesus was demonstrating an example of God's embrace. Of course, we're compelled to ask, how can suffering show God's love for us? Believe it or not, frequently, things that happen to us aren't punishment by God for our actions. On the contrary, God is reaching out to us and embracing us with an opportunity to grow in faith.

It's the paradox of life that in suffering, we often find God. Yet at the same time, in suffering, we also find an absence of God. Truly it doesn't make sense. It's important for us to pay attention to these times in our lives.

Several years ago, for a number of reasons, my career opportunities suddenly declined. I blamed God! My first question was,

"What have I done to deserve this punishment?" I had been able to create a good standard of living for my family and me. It was being threatened, and the things I had worked so hard for were actually disappearing right before me. Although it was very painful and difficult, I came to realize through the study of the Scriptures that this was an opportunity for me to look deeper into myself. An opportunity to see what God might be calling me to do as a result of this change in life.

I began to see it more as an embrace from God. It sounds funny, but soon I began to fear that suddenly things would get better, the problems would resolve, and I would lose the closeness that I was enjoying with God.

Of course, I'm not suggesting that you seek out the negative sides of life to find God, because, truly, it's in those situations that we can't find God. We cry out to hear from God, assuring us that in just a moment…"everything will be all right." Jesus himself, when hanging on the cross in his moment of deepest despair, felt that God had abandoned him. He cried to his very own Father, "Why hast thou forsaken me?" Of course, there was no answer. Even Jesus understood that God wouldn't spare him because of who he was, for Jesus was carrying out God's greater purpose.

In our pain and suffering, there comes the potential for wisdom. Realize that life will never be perfect.

Don't judge yourself for the negative things that happen to you and others. We will find our lives aren't always what we want them to be. We must see others and ourselves as Jesus sees us. We're human beings on the path. We're on a journey to fulfill our created purpose. In doing this, Ignatius said, we must not care about external things like health or sickness, wealth or poverty, fame or obscurity, a long life or a short one. That is the third principle of Ignatius. We must focus on our purpose for life and use whatever happens to us, good or not so good, to learn what our true life and purpose is all about. When bad things happen to good people, stop and think that it might very well be God embracing them to help them recognize an opportunity to draw closer to him.

Have you ever found yourself questioning someone's actions, perhaps thinking that his or her misfortune must be a result of poor choices he or she made? That is often the furthest thing from the truth. If you're going through difficult or painful times yourself, warranted or not, be willing to walk through them and allow God to prepare you for what or how he plans to use you as part of his purpose for you.

Make Your Requests Known

Now that you've read the reflection and imagine yourself as one of Jesus' disciples asking if the man's blindness was punishment for sin, write a brief answer to each question. Realize that the answers are yours alone. Give yourself freedom to write whatever comes to mind about the world, about whatever suffering you've experienced. Let your mind go to the full feelings and understanding of where you are in terms of the question. Remember, at times you're writing what you say to Jesus. At other times, you'll find yourself writing what Jesus says to you. Date the conversation. If, while you're answering one of the questions provided, another question comes to you, write it down. Feel free to add your own questions. Again today, God, I ask you for clarity. There are so many things I don't understand. I seek to put my life in your hands. I seek to understand why bad things happen to good people. My tendency is to think that you're punishing them or me. You know that I sometimes pray for what is happening to me to go away and that my life gets better, rather than praying to understand what I need to learn as a result of my suffering.

- *How today can I see Jesus in myself and those around me?*
- *How today can I understand that when I suffer, it's part of God's embrace?*
- *What wisdom do I need to gain when things don't go the way I want them to?*

Help me to pray to seek wisdom in my suffering, rather than pray that my suffering be alleviated.

Engage Jesus in Conversation

Now, direct the questions that you couldn't answer and the questions that you came up with on your own, to Jesus, sitting there with you. Ask him for insights into what you wrote down. Ask him for clarity. Ask him to help you see the world as he does. Ask him how to use your gifts to understand what happens to you and those you love. Ask him to help you dig deeply into the activities of this day and acknowledge that whatever the outcomes are, you'll do all things in His honor and glory and in appreciation for what he has given you to pass on to others.

Offer Thanks—Closing Prayer

Ask Jesus to be involved in your day. Ask him to give you guidance. Ask him to help you see within all you observe, where he is asking you to help Lazarus. Ask him to help you understand in the experiences you have today how he is reaching out to you. To see in the people you connect with how Jesus is guiding you.

Dear God, I appreciate so much all you've done for me. I appreciate it when things go the way I want, and I'm trying to appreciate it when things don't go the way I want. I seek to understand what you're trying to get me to understand when life isn't what I desire. Help me to pause and seek to see Jesus in myself and others. Help me today to stay strong in my weakness and to continue to seek answers within my suffering and the suffering of those I love. I'm beginning to realize that suffering often reveals the true wisdom in life and the true definition of your purpose for me. Amen.

Evening Examen

Today you were gaining insights into the meaning of pain and frustration. It's important to ask the "what," not necessarily the "why" of pain and suffering. When things don't go our way, we get stuck in wanting to know why this happened rather than what we should be gaining from it. Today's example of the blind man helped you understand into how not only the good, but also the bad, can bring you to a deeper understanding and faith.

Pause—Gain Interior Peace

In spite of the rigors of your day, it's time to quiet yourself again. It's time to move away from all the stuff, away from the tension. This is special time to still yourself to get a clearer understanding of where Jesus was coming to you. As you sit quietly by yourself, open yourself to listen to the voice within. Close your eyes for a few moments or focus your eyes on an object for a brief period of time.

Enter—Practice the Presence—Face to Face

Jesus is present with you. Place yourself in his presence. Think about him sitting there beside you. Think about how much he knows about you; think about all the insights he has about how your day has been. Today, he was very active in your life. Each of us wants to understand where the Lord speaks to us, and what he is saying. Each day, you become more sensitive to his presence.

Begin With Silent Prayer

O, Lord, today was a day of challenge to see the meaning of pain and suffering. Help me to understand what I'm to learn when things don't go my way. Give me insights as to what I'm called to do as a result of the pain I experience in myself and the pain I see in others' lives. In all of this, I seek to understand what it's that I should do in order to give honor and glory to you through those around me. I know that you're with me. I know that you care about me and are leading me to serve in your name. I have come to realize that pain and suffering aren't determined by a person's sins, but rather, by the circumstances of the world. My world seems to be in so much pain. It's hard not to blame you. Help me keep it all in perspective. Come into my heart and my mind in these next few minutes and break down the barriers of confusion. Open me to the messages you gave today. Amen.

Reflect—Use Your Imagination

Think about the people you met and the things you experienced today. Each day brings both challenges and joys. Both bring you insights into the presence of the Lord. Both give you insights where you should focus your efforts toward seeking understanding of pain and suffering. Remember, the Lord is with you always. You're coming to recognize his hand in your life, guiding you to understand what he is calling you to do. What happened today that stood out in your mind? What could you have done that you didn't do?

Make Your Requests Known

Write a brief answer to each of the following questions. Write whatever comes to mind. Let your mind go to the full feeling and understanding of where you are in terms of the question. More of your answers are coming from Jesus and fewer from you. If another question comes to you, write it down. Your own questions will get you to a deeper level of reflection and conversation with the Lord.

As part of your reflection, ask Jesus these questions.

- *Today, I had so much opportunity to enjoy the good things. I had an opportunity to learn from the things that weren't so good.*
- *Lord, where today, did I find a deeper understanding of life through my pain?*
- *Who did I meet that reflected Jesus' attitudes about life?*
- *What can I acknowledge as a message from God in my experiences?*
- *What did I do today that brought me energy in my activities?*
- *What one thing happened today that became my theme for the day and drew me closer to an understanding of myself and of God's purpose for me?*

Engage Jesus in Conversation

Now, share your answers with Jesus. Read them out loud if you can. Ask him agreement to what you wrote down. At times, he will gently disagree and give you additional insights that will bring you to a deeper understanding of where you are in relationship to today's experiences.

> *O, Lord, am I asking the right questions? Where in my answers have I missed your message? Am I finding clarity in what you're saying to me? What should I do to recognize your presence in whom I meet and what I experience?*

Offer Thanks—Closing Prayer

> *Thanks Jesus for special insights and grace he gave you today. O, Lord, thank you for all the grace you gave me today. Without you, I can do nothing and with you, I can focus on serving others in your name. Thank you for the insights I have gained during this reflection. Thank you for the clarity I seek to understand where pain and suffering bring meaning to my journey. Thank you for opening my eyes to the suffering of those around me. I know that you'll continue to help me better understand what you're calling me to do. I offer this and all my actions to your greater honor and glory. Amen.*

Seventh Encounter

Want What You Were Created For

Morning Reflection

Pause—Gain Interior Peace

As you come to the seventh encounter of your journey, move to quiet yourself to hear his voice. This has become something that you look forward to, but it still requires a commitment. The business and rush of life draw you away from the Lord. Remember, Jesus isn't in a rush. He is with you the rest of your life. Separate yourself from thinking about all that you need to do today. Listen to the voice within. Find an object that gets your attention and focus on it briefly, or simply close your eyes and peer into the nothingness of your vision.

Enter—Practice Dwelling in the Presence of Jesus—Face to Face

Focus on his presence. He is there. He is always there. You have come to know that, as you reflect with him. You have been getting clearer insights into things that happen to you. He is bringing you joy, as you come to see your purpose in this world. Total fulfillment in this life isn't possible, but every day you're provided with the tools to develop a deeper relationship with him. Sometimes, it's a person; at other times, it's a situation. It might even be a desire that he places in your heart that will serve his Father's purpose on earth. If you want what you were created for, you come to realize his presence in all you meet; you'll come to see how everything works together. Jesus is listening. He offers insights into what you'll encounter today. Jesus will guide you to know and want what you were created for.

He leans forward as he speaks to you...

When you're with me, time doesn't rush by quickly for you. I have eternity. We will be together forever. Isn't that wonderful? It's only the world that is passing away. You and I won't pass away. You'll still frequently miss opportunities to serve my mission on earth, if you continue placing emphasis on doing things. You're no longer a river rushing shallow everywhere. You're becoming a well, deep with capacity, that won't run out. You must want what you were created for and nothing else.

You're still concerned that you'll miss where I'm directing you. Move forward, reaching out to the community. I have prepared you to live the Scripture so that others can apply it to their daily lives. I'm preparing you to bring the light of faith to all those you encounter.

*How often have you heard something or read something that you didn't get a spiritual connection from? There are spiritual insights from everything because everything has a spiritual connection. You're created to be a connector. I inspire you through the people and experiences that I give you. When the world doesn't inspire you in the same way, look to me. **Stay with me!** Stand still with **me!** Today is another special day. You'll experience amazing things. The challenge at this point in the journey is to stay the course. Respect the time we have together. Bring the things you're doing in the world to me. Then our relationship will be seamless.*

Begin With Silent Prayer

O, Lord, I understand that I have failed in my life to focus effectively on what I was created for. I realize that in my humble reflection, I have sought to fill my life with "doing" rather than "being"; with things that I collect or obtain rather than what I have come to be in terms of your service. Please help me to become clearer about what you've created me for. Help me identify the pearl of great value in my life. Help me to always ask myself if the things I do and the things I have acquired make me happy? Do the riches I've gained, make me happy? Do they help me know you and love others? Amen.

Reflect—Use Your Imagination

Place yourself in the situation that you're about to read. Put yourself into the Scripture about the rich merchant who was willing to direct all his efforts on the pearl. Think about how Jesus is bringing you to understand you pearl of great wisdom. Think about the excitement of the merchant, who discovers the pearl and realizes its value.

Again, the kingdom of heaven is like a merchant in search of fine pearls; on finding one pearl of great value, he went and sold all that he had and bought it.

MATTHEW 13:45–46

Each of us is created for a reason, not reasons. Most of us confuse our lives by focusing on all the things we need to do, all the things we need to gain, all the things we need to accomplish, rather than the thing for which we were created, like the pearl of great value. Saint Augustine wrote, "You have made us for yourself, O, Lord, and our heart is restless until it rests in you." His profound wisdom is something we all need to reflect upon.

First, that which we were created for was to live a life destined to be with God. A life destined to earn salvation. So many of us start our day out like this: we get out of bed and begin making daily lists of things we need to get done before our first cup of coffee. We live our day around that list. Some of us have even taken classes on how to prioritize the list so that we make sure the things vital to accomplishment are at the top. Others of us live our lives in blocks, designed so that we can accomplish something each and every hour.

A friend of mine named Joseph lived a long life full of accomplishment, or accomplishing things. He had three pages that listed all the things he had accomplished in his life from president of this organization, to founder of that organization, to the planes he had acquired, to the trips he had taken, even down to the children he had fathered. But if someone had looked at the list and asked, "What was the one thing?" it would be hard to identify the purpose for Joseph's life. It was hard for Joseph to identify the purpose for his life, himself, but he certainly was busy 24/7.

Many of us are like Joseph. Confusion about our life's purpose derails us and keeps us from finding true joy. We get confused as to purpose for doing and doing for purpose. Consider this—is our purpose veiled in lots of activity, just getting things done, or does the purpose initiate the doing?

In other words, have we identified that one thing for which we were created and are we "doing" an outcome of that purpose? For example, the purpose can be as simple as organizing people to serve, hopefully to serve God or others. The activities are then directed to that end. This truth applies to anyone, a doctor, housekeeper, teacher, mechanic or cook. Any job, career, or task can be founded on that purpose.

> *Yet whatever gains I had, these I have come to regard as loss because of Christ. More than that, I regard everything as loss because of the surpassing value of knowing Christ Jesus my Lord. For his sake I have suffered the loss of all things, and I regard them as rubbish, in order that I may gain Christ...*
>
> PHILIPPIANS 3:7–8

Two questions should arise in our reflection. First, of all the things we do that make us rich, do they make us happy? Second, do they help us know God and to love people?

If you can answer yes to both of these questions, then the things that have made you rich are good. If not, then quite simply, they aren't.

Make Your Requests Known

Now that you've read the reflection and imagined yourself as one of Jesus' disciples asking how one can come to know what the pearl is in their life, write a brief answer to each question. Realize that the answers are yours alone. Give yourself freedom to write whatever comes to mind about purpose and meaning. Let your mind go to the full feelings and understanding of where you are in terms of the question. Remember, at times, you're writing what you say to Jesus. At other times, you'll find yourself writing what Jesus says to you. Date the conversation. If, while you're answering one of the questions provided, another question comes to you, write it down. Feel free to add your own questions.

Lord, I ask you for clarity. There are so many things I don't understand. I seek to put my life in your hands. I seek to understand what the pearl of my life is, the purpose for which I was created. You know that as I get closer to the meaning of the pearl, I'll resist wanting it so much that I'm willing to give up other things for its possession. I pray that you help me to be open to an understanding and a desire for want of what I was created for.

- *Lord, how can I discover in my life the pearl that is worth giving everything up for?*
- *How can I realize in my daily experiences which activities I do that lead me to the fulfillment of my created purpose?*
- *How can I come to live a life more in tune with what you've created me for?*
- *What will I do today that truly makes me happy?*
- *What will I do today that will help me know God and love people?*
- *How can I take the time today to reflect, rather than just do?*

Engage Jesus in Conversation

Now, direct the questions that you couldn't answer and the questions that you came up with on your own, to Jesus, sitting there with you. Ask him for insights into what you wrote down. Ask him for clarity. Ask him to help you see the meaning in what is happening to you. Ask him to help you dig deeply into the activities of this day and acknowledge that whatever the outcomes are, you'll do all things in his honor and glory and in appreciation for what he has given you to pass on to others.

Offer Thanks—Closing Prayer

Ask Jesus to be involved in your day. Ask him to give you guidance. Ask him to help you see within all you observe, where he is showing you your pearl. Ask him to help you understand in the experiences you have today how he is reaching out to you.

Dear Lord, thank you for giving me this time to reflect, time for getting close to you and to seek understanding for my created purpose. I know that there is a pearl of great value in my life. Help me to understand by shedding many of the activities of my life, I'll find truer joy and happiness in serving you and loving others. Help me today to stay focused, to pause before I rush into activity. Help me to be clear about what I'm doing in relationship to who I'm and how I serve you more fully. I'm beginning to realize that it's not the number of things I get done, but the relationship of those activities to my true purpose that brings me energy and joy. Amen.

Evening Examen

Today you were gaining insights into the meaning of wanting only what Jesus wants for you life. The majority of each day, unfortunately, focuses on what the world demands of you. It fights for your time and attention. Your relationship with Christ and what he wants of you slips away from the focus of your effort. Often, we come to question where Jesus' purpose for our lives fits in all the other things. In truth, it fits into everything. God created everything, and everything God made in the image of Jesus Christ. But you must cooperate with his presence. Everything is co-redemptive but just as Augustine says with grace: for it to be effective, you must open yourself to it. To come to want what Christ wants for you, you must first know, then understand and then cooperate; that means participate. As Saint Paul said in his letter to the Colossians:

> *And whatever you do, in word or deed, do everything in the name of the Lord Jesus, giving thanks to God the Father through him.*

COLOSSIANS 3:17

Pause—Gain Interior Peace

In spite of the challenges of this day, it's time to quiet yourself again. It's time to move away from all the stuff, away from the tension, away from the temptations of the world. This is special time to still yourself to get a clearer understanding of where Jesus came to you today. As you sit quietly by yourself, open yourself to listen to the voice within. Close your eyes for a few moments or focus on a single object for a brief time.

Enter—Practice the Presence—Face to Face

Jesus is present. Think about him sitting there beside you. He knows everything about you. He was with you all day, even when you didn't know it. He sees the whole plan for your future. Each day, you've become more sensitive to his presence.

Begin With Silent Prayer

O, Lord, today was a day of challenge to see what you want for my life. Help me to understand what I'm to learn. Give me insights as to what I'm called to do as a result of the experiences I had and the people I met. In all of this, I seek to understand what it's that I should do that gives honor and glory to your purpose for my life. I know that you're with me. I know that you care about me and are leading me to serve in your name. I'm coming to realize that the more I want what you want for me, the deeper our relationship and the more joy and fulfillment I experience. Come into my heart and my mind in these next few minutes, and break down the barriers of confusion. Open me to your messages you gave today. Amen.

Reflect—Use Your Imagination

Think about the people you met and the things that you experienced today. Each day brings both challenges and joys. Both bring you insights into what the Lord want you to do in your life. Both give you insights into where you should focus your efforts toward paradise. Remember, the Lord is with you always. You're coming to recognize his hand in your life, guiding you to understand what he is calling you to do each day—how to love, how to give, how to share hope, how to understand pain and suffering.

- *What happened today that stood out in your mind?*
- *Where did you encounter someone with a message for you?*
- *What could you have done that you didn't do?*

Make Your Requests Known

Now write a brief answer to each of the following questions. Give yourself freedom to write whatever comes to mind. Let your mind go to the full feelings and understanding of where you are in terms of the question. You're noticing that more of your answers are coming from Jesus and fewer from you. If, while you're writing, another question comes to you, write it down. You have found that your own questions will get you to a deeper level of reflection and conversation with the Lord.

Today was a day of joy. Today was a day that, even in my frustrations, I found some clarity. Good things happened to me today. Again, I had the opportunity to learn from the things that happened, whether they were good or bad.

- *When today did I have insights that helped me understand my purpose?*
- *What things happened to me today that gave me energy?*
- *Where today did I experience things that gave me joy?*
- *Who brought me insights as to my true role in life, my pearl?*
- *What did I do today that led me back into my old self, the self that was full of doing things so I could check them off the list?*
- *What was one thing that happened today that became my theme and drew me closer to an understanding of my true purpose?*

Engage Jesus in Conversation

Now, share your answers with Jesus. Read them out loud if you can. Ask him for agreement to what you wrote down. At times, he will gently disagree and give you additional insights that will bring you to a deeper understanding of where you are in relationship to today's experiences.

O, Lord, am I asking the right questions? Where in my answers have I missed your message? Am I finding clarity in what you're saying to me? What I should do recognize your presence in who I meet and what I experience?

Offer Thanks—Closing Prayer

Thank Jesus for special insights and grace he gave you today.

O, Lord, thank you for all the grace you gave me today. Without you, I can do nothing and with you, I can focus on serving in your name. Thank you for the insights I have gained during this reflection. Thank you for the clarity that I seek to understand where pain and suffering bring meaning to my journey with you. Thank you for opening my eyes to everything around me. I know that you'll continue to help me better understand what you're calling me to do. I offer this and all my actions to your greater honor and glory. Amen.

Conclusion

L
ife is a journey of self-discovery and the search for meaning in each of our lives. Created with meaning and purpose, we each have an innate drive particular to each of us. Understanding of our life purpose comes only with an ever-deepening relationship with Christ. Each step, as we get out of our boat of life and walk with Christ, brings us to special encounters. Insights resulting from these encounters guides us on the path of life.

The longer the journey and the closer we stay to the path, our lives converge seamlessly with the clear point of life. If you've completed the seven encounters with Christ, you're out of the boat and beginning to discover the messages that come with each encounter and experience. Your relationship is for eternity; the joy comes in the process that brings us to our created purpose and everlasting life.

However, like when we learned to take our first steps or ride a bicycle or sail a boat, we're going to fall down or get wet. Our advantage comes from the fall, which stems from finding our lives stretched too far. This fall gives us the opportunity to get up again.

In getting up, we come to know our Lord in the most intimate way. Remember, our all-loving Lord will not remember the depth of our mistakes but rather the quality and frequency of our recovery.

About the Author

Thomas Winninger is the founder of Winninger Resource Companies, Inc., a Minneapolis-based group that provides products, services, and technologies that drive market leadership based on intentional strategic planning.

He is a recipient of the Cavett Award, the National Speakers Association's highest award, which is given annually to a person who gives back to the industry by sharing his time, talent, and gifts. In 1987 Thom was inducted into the NSA's Council of Peers Award for Excellence Speaker Hall of Fame.

Thom is a permanent deacon at St. Olaf Catholic Church in Minneapolis, Minnesota.

Contact Thom through his website, www.winninger.com, or via e-mail thomas@winninger.com.